Making Peace
with Your Past

Facilitator Guide

Tim Sledge

LifeWay Press®
Nashville, Tennessee

ISBN: 0-8054-9987-3
Item: 001117296

Dewey Decimal Classification: 259.4

Subject Heading: CHURCH WORK WITH THE HURTING \\ DYSFUNCTIONAL FAMILIES

To order additional copies of this resource:
WRITE LifeWay Church Resources Customer Service;
One LifeWay Plaza; Nashville, TN 37234-0113;
FAX order to (615) 251-5933; PHONE (800) 458-2772;
E-MAIL *orderentry@lifeway.com;*
or VISIT the LifeWay Christian Store serving you.

Printed in the United States of America

Leadership and Adult Publishing
LifeWay Church Resources
One LifeWay Plaza
Nashville, TN 37234-0175

Contents

Introduction

All across America people are seeking out small support groups for help in dealing with problems. Churches are beginning to realize that they must minister to these deeply personal needs of both church members and people in the community. As churches provide Christ-centered support groups, the gospel takes on relevance as people experience the redemptive and healing work of Jesus Christ.

Lay-led support groups can be very beneficial. *Making Peace with Your Past* is designed for use in lay-led support groups called Face-to-Face Support Groups. These are not therapy groups but are Christ-centered sharing groups that help people deal with issues related to their family of origin. *Making Peace with Your Past* is a part of the LIFE® Support Group Series.

What Is the LIFE® Support Group Series?

The LIFE® Support Group Series is an educational system of Discovery Group and Support Group resources for providing Christian ministry and emotional support to individuals in areas of social, emotional, and physical need. Issues dealt with include such things as divorce recovery, grief, chemical dependency, codependency, abuse recovery, eating disorders, and so forth.

The LIFE® Support Group Series provides resources for two types of group processes. The Discovery Group studies dysfunctional family issues and other problem areas that individuals might face. A *group leader* guides discussion of the topics and helps group members consider applications to life. Though persons naturally will get in touch with emotions, feelings, and personal problems, Discovery Groups focus on discussion of the content in the member book. These groups generally are less emotionally intense and require less skill and training of the leader. For that reason they provide safe and excellent starting points for support group ministries in a church. *Search for Significance* LIFE® Support Group Series Edition, *Untangling Relationships*, and *Breaking the Cycle of Hurtful Family Experiences* are discovery group resources that will meet many needs.

A Support Group is composed of people who meet because of personal issues common to group members. Support Groups focus on helping members gain awareness; understanding; and emotional, psychological, and spiritual support for dealing with personal life issues. LIFE® Support Group Series resources provide help for three types of support groups:

1. Encouragement and Accountability Support Group where members encourage and support each other's progress toward a goal. A discovery-group level of leadership skills is sufficient for this type of support group. *Fit 4: A LifeWay Christian Wellness Plan* is a resource for this type of support group.

2. Personal Issues Support Group where members share personal responses to issues and problems with which they are dealing. *Making Peace with Your Past* and *Moving Beyond Your Past* are resources for personal-issues support groups related to family of origin issues. Such groups need a skilled *lay facilitator* for a Personal Issues Support Group because of the volatile emotions that may erupt in the group sessions.

3. 12-Step Support Group where members use a Christian adaptation of Alcoholics Anonymous' 12 Steps to help each other make progress in recovery from addictions through a process of repentance, trust in God, and spiritual renewal. Twelve-Step Support Groups also require a skilled lay facilitator to manage the group sessions. *Conquering Chemical Dependency*, *Conquering Codependency*, and *Conquering Eating Disorders* are resources for use in these groups.

Facilitating a Face-to-Face Group

Not every group leader is capable of facilitating a Face-to-Face Support Group. Special skills and experiences are required. If you have not led intensive support group sessions before, read through the criteria for a facilitator on page 5. Do not try to lead a Face-to-Face group until you have the training and skill necessary to deal with the problems that can arise in the group sessions.

If you do meet the criteria, the following material will help you prepare for your Face-to-Face Support Group. Complete the steps recommended for starting a group and study carefully the Basic Skills for Group Leadership. Make prayer a major part of your preparation. Seek God's help throughout this process and give glory to Him for all the good things that take place in the lives of participants.

Steps for Starting a Face-to-Face Support Group

The following steps can help you prepare for effectively ministering through Face-to-Face Support Groups.

Step 1: Orienting to the Course Content

✎ **Check each of the following as you complete your overview.**

❑ Steps for Starting a Face-to-Face Support Group
❑ Goals for a Face-to-Face Support Group
❑ Foundational Concepts for the Group Process
❑ Basic Skills for Group Leadership
❑ Training Potential Group Facilitators
❑ Weekly Session Guides 1-12
❑ *Making Peace with Your Past* member book

Read this book and the member book, *Making Peace with Your Past*. Be certain that you understand the goals for the group (see "Goals for a Face-to-Face Support Group," beginning on p. 10 in this guide). Reading the materials will give you an idea of what will occur during the sessions. It will make you feel more confident in your leadership role.

Step 2: Determine Whether You Are Equipped to Lead a Face-to-Face Support Group

This is a crucial step. Not every group facilitator is ready to lead a support group. Because members will be dealing with potentially intense and volatile emotions, you need to be prepared to handle these emotions appropriately.

You need to know how to handle emotionally volatile issues. The emotional health and perhaps even the lives of some members will be at stake.
In evaluating your potential as a facilitator, first consider some basic qualities that a facilitator should have. A facilitator should:

> You must be an equipped facilitator before attempting to lead a Face-to-Face Support Group.

1. Be a growing Christian, a person of prayer, and a person who has faith in what God can do
2. Possess Christian values
3. Be an active member of a local church
4. Sense God's call to be involved in ministry
5. Be spiritually gifted for the work
6. Have a knowledge of Scripture
7. Be able to relate well to people
8. Commit to keep confidential information private
9. Be willing to give time and energy to help members of the group
10. Have a teachable spirit
11. Be in the process of overcoming personal experience with a painful past
12. Be emotionally stable

Persons who have led groups through *MasterLife, Disciple's Prayer Life,* or *Experiencing God* should have strong spiritual foundations for facilitating a support group. However, besides these spiritual foundations, they also need some skills to guide the group process successfully.

Some of the skills needed are addressed in the "Basic Skills for Group Leadership." Two other very important skills are (1) knowing how to help a person who indicates a tendency toward self-destructive or suicidal behavior and (2) knowing how to make a referral to an appropriate Christian counselor or Christ-centered institution when a person needs help beyond your gifts and abilities. Helps with these two skills and with a variety of other lay counseling skills can be developed in a group process of studying *Wise Counsel: Skills for Lay Counseling.* Other helps are provided in *LIFE Support Leader Handbook* (see p. 18).

Most group facilitation skills, however, are difficult to learn by reading a book. They are learned best by experiencing them under the leadership of a skilled support-group facilitator. If you have not learned these skills in a group process, consider one of the following suggestions for developing the necessary skills:

1. Participate as a group member of a Face-to-Face Support Group being offered in your church or in another church.
2. Participate in some other type of intensive support group process for a period of time.
3. Attend an intensive training event where skilled facilitators help you see, develop, and practice support-group facilitation skills.

Please do not attempt to facilitate a Face-to-Face Support Group without preparation. If you do, members could have an experience that causes more harm than good. A bad group experience could abort your church's support-group ministry because your church could fear getting involved in the process again.

This warning is not designed to scare you. It is intended to keep unprepared facilitators from getting into crises for which they are unprepared.

Step 3: Secure Approval from Your Church's Leadership

If you are a layperson, be sure to consult the appropriate church-staff member before scheduling a Face-to-Face Support Group in your church. Provide the staff member a copy of this facilitator guide and of the member book. Make sure that the staff member understands what will happen in the group, goals, content, and procedures. Attempt to answer any questions the staff member may have. Give the staff member time to review the materials before you ask for approval to go ahead with the course. If you are unsure about whether you are qualified to be a facilitator, ask the staff person to help you evaluate your skills.

If you are a church-staff member, consider reviewing the aims of the course with appropriate lay leaders before you proceed. Be certain that lay leaders understand that the course is a Bible-based approach to dysfunctional-family issues.

The *LIFE Support Leader Handbook* provides guidance for beginning and guiding a group ministry. The *Handbook* can be downloaded at no charge from *http://www.lifeway.com/download.asp*.

Step 4: Order Materials

Order sufficient copies of the following materials well in advance of your first meeting.
- Member book (item 0-8054-9986-5), one copy for each group member
- Facilitator guide (item 0-8054-9987-3), one copy for your apprentice

To purchase materials: Write LifeWay Church Resources Customer Service; One LifeWay Plaza; Nashville, TN 37234-0113; Fax order to (615) 251.5933; Phone (800) 458-2772; Email to *customerservice@lifeway.com*; Order online at *www.lifeway.com*; or Visit the LifeWay Christian Store serving you.

Step 5: Set Fees

Each group member should pay for his or her own book. You may want to charge an additional materials fee to help cover related costs for this ministry. For example, you might use the additional fees collected to provide scholarships for persons who cannot buy their own materials, or to purchase leadership materials.

Asking each group member to pay a fee helps communicate the level of commitment expected of group members. We often avoid charging persons for courses because we do not want them to feel that we are trying to make a profit. However, people tend to be suspicious of things that are free. "What's the catch?" is their question. Charging a small fee for materials and other expenses actually can lessen unchurched persons' apprehensions about participating in the group.

To protect your church from legal liability, do not charge fees or pay the facilitator for group leadership. This is a lay-led group, not a professional-led group.

Step 6: Begin Skill Building

Study carefully the section "Basic Skills for Group Leadership" in this book.

Step 7: Enlist an Apprentice

Pray about finding someone who will go through the group as a participant but who also displays a willingness to lead a group later. You may choose this person from those individuals who sign up for the group, or you may want to enlist someone who appears to have the appropriate skills for facilitating a group, even though he or she did not sign up for the study. Training the proper apprentice is highly important.

Step 8: Set a Date and Time for Starting

Ideally, the study should be offered when the group sessions will not be disturbed by interruptions such as holidays. A registration period of at least three weeks is suggested. Registration should end one week before the first session since group members are asked to complete five daily assignments before the first session.

If you decide to offer Face-to-Face Support Groups year-round, a good schedule is to start one group in early fall, one group in January, and another group in late spring or early summer. This provides enough time between each study to handle registration and preparation for the next group. It also gives group facilitators a needed break.

Set a starting time that will be most convenient for group members. You will need to allow at least two hours for each session.

Step 9: Find a Place to Meet

The group should meet in the same place each week. The room in which the group meets should be quiet and private enough that members feel free to talk and even shout when they express intense emotions.

Avoid a location where children will be running through a nearby hallway or peeking through the door. Such an atmosphere will make group members anxious and unwilling to share. The best meeting place usually is in the church building at a time when few other activities are in progress. Meeting in a person's home is not recommended.

A room with an entrance away from the main entrance to the church building is helpful. Members need to be able to come and go without worrying that others will ask them where they have been or what they were doing.

Group members often cry during a session. Often women stop wearing makeup to the sessions after meeting several times because they anticipate crying. Group members need to be able to leave the session without worrying about being seen after they obviously have been crying.

The room should be large enough to hold a circle of about eight chairs comfortably. The room should be clean and comfortable. Windows are OK unless they are positioned so that passersby can look inside and make group members feel uncomfortable. Restrooms should be accessible to the meeting room.

Step 10: Decide on Child Care

Decide whether you will provide child care. The advantage of offering child care is that it may enable some persons to come who could not participate otherwise. The disadvantage is that support-group sessions sometimes run late. You need the freedom to let the session last a little longer if a group member is doing significant sharing. Child care could become a handicap if group members feel the need to leave the session early to take children home. The best solution usually is for group members to secure child care on their own.

Step 11: Advertise the Group

How should you let others know about the group? First, decide on the target audience. I recommend that you structure the group for unchurched persons as well as for members of your church. Many who attend our groups are not members of our church. Often they join our church as a result of participating in a group.

Many persons in your community who have attended secular recovery groups are looking for a Christian recovery group. Often the groups these persons have attended have helped, but they hunger for a group in which such persons freely can integrate their Christian faith with the principles of recovery.

Place an advertisement in your local paper. Words like *recovery, dysfunctional families,* and *adult children* will catch the attention of potential group members. Mention that enrollment is limited and will be accepted on a first-come, first-served basis. Announce the fact that the group has formed in your church. Use the church newsletter to advertise the group.

Once you complete your first group, word-of-mouth comments represent your strongest publicity. A successful group will lead new persons to request information about the next group.

Be sure to have a phone number available by which interested persons always can get specific information about when the next group will be offered. Designate one person to receive all inquiries about the group. This ensures that callers receive accurate information and helps build trust. Confidential issues frequently are shared during the initial inquiry about the group. Once a group starts, other persons may express an interest. The Face-to-Face Support Group is a closed group. No one can be added to the group after the first session. Begin registration for your second group as soon as one person commits to lead it. You may find that you have a full group before the first group has finished the study.

Step 12: Interview Prospective Group Members

What is the minimum number of persons needed for the group to function well? The dynamics of the group should operate properly if you have at least three persons in addition to yourself. The group should contain no more than eight persons. If the group fills up, record additional names and start another group when you have enough persons and a qualified facilitator.
Each person who expresses an interest in being a member of the group should meet with you. During this discussion give the member a copy of the book *Making Peace with Your Past* and cover the following points.

Discuss the goals for the group. Discuss the group's goals listed in the introduction in the member book. Talk about the group's purpose. Ask whether participants have any questions about the purpose.

Explain that spouses should be in separate groups. If a person's spouse also is interested in participating, explain that he or she will need to be in a separate group (see concept 8, p. 17).

Explain the covenant. Review the covenant that follows the introduction in the member book. Explain that one must be willing to sign the covenant to participate in the group. Ask if participants have any questions about the covenant. Ask the individual to sign the covenant in your presence. You may want to keep a signed copy on file. If you do, take a photocopy with you for signing.

Explain daily assignments. Review the daily assignments for unit 1 in the member book. Explain that participating in the group requires the individual to be willing to spend between 30 and 60 minutes a day, five days a week, working on the assignments. Tell the prospective group member that the five assignments should not all be done on one day each week. Because many of the assignments are reflective, participants should complete them in daily segments rather than back-to-back in one day. Explain that participants should complete the assignments for unit 1 before they begin the first session.

Discuss a commitment. The individual may immediately commit to participating in the group. If so, ask her to sign the covenant in her book. Keep a copy of the signed covenant for your records. Record the person's name, address, phone number, and church affiliation.

Ask for permission to include this person's name and phone number on a roster that will be distributed to the group. If the person is uncomfortable with this request, do not force the issue.

Write the date, day, time, and place of the first session on a sheet of paper and give it to the registrant.

If the individual wants to think about her decision to participate in the group, encourage her to do so. Let her know how to contact you when she makes the decision. If the group is nearly full (a maximum size of eight persons including yourself is recommended), let her know that other persons may register and that the group soon may be full. Inform this person of the final deadline for group registration (usually one week before the first session).
Be sensitive in determining whether a financial problem is making it impossible for someone to purchase the book. When possible, offer help. Avoid turning anyone away because of a lack of money. Scholarships always should be available if needed.

Reassure the prospective group member. Explain that at no time will any group member be forced to do or say anything against his will. Group members will be lovingly challenged to confront the pain of the past but always will have freedom of choice about what they do. Remember that the thought of sharing about a painful childhood is very frightening. Be sensitive to this fear and use the initial interview as a time to begin creating a sense of trust with this person.

Tell the person that it is not unusual to feel afraid. Offer to pray for him as he prepares for the first session. Make yourself available to answer any further questions.

Step 13: Prepare a Group Roster and Name Tags

When you have completed registration, make a roster that includes all group members who have given you permission to record their names and phone numbers on the list. Make a copy for each person in the group.

Make another list, adding the names of any group members who did not give permission to include their names on the shared roster. Use it to record attendance of the group members.

A person who misses more than two sessions may be asked to drop out of the group. The members of the group will make this decision.

Prepare a reusable name tag for each group member. Include first and last names. Face-to-Face Support Groups are confidential but not anonymous. Plan to distribute the name tags at the beginning of each session and to take them up at the end of each session.

Step 14: Pray for Each Group Member

Begin praying regularly for each group member. Pray especially that God will remove any fears each may have about the first session. Pray that God will help you lead the group effectively.

Step 15: Begin the Sessions

The first session of a Face-to-Face Support Group is an exciting event. You will sense anticipation, as well as some fear, when you walk into the room for the first session. You will learn more about what happens during the first session in Part 2 of this book. Follow the instructions in "Before the Session" on page 32 to prepare for the first session.

Step 16: Plan for Follow-up Groups

During session 10 you will begin to discuss options for follow-up groups. Your church's overall support group ministry may influence which of the following options you offer for discussion. Begin now to make plans for follow-up groups. Many members will need continuing

---

Important: Few (if any) group members will be able to process all the issues raised in this course during 12 weeks. You must provide for follow-up opportunities to begin at the end of this 12-week course.

---

support after the first 12 weeks of studying *Making Peace with Your Past*.

Possible options include:

- Review group–Your existing Face-to-Face group could agree to meet together for 12 more weeks. Members could review content in *Making Peace with Your Past* and use the sharing-only format for the group sessions. This would be a good time to share leadership and provide on-the-job training for potential leaders.
- New content/same group–Your existing group could agree to stay together for another 12 weeks and to use

Search for Significance LIFE® Support Group Series Edition or *Untangling Relationships* as additional input for group members.
- New Face-to-Face groups–Members can go through the Face-to-Face process in new groups. These groups could include both experienced and first-time participants.
- *Moving Beyond Your Past* groups– Members may choose to continue his or her growth by forming a *Moving Beyond Your Past* group. *Moving Beyond Your Past* helps adults move beyond the hurts of the past into a life of joy, purpose, and meaning.
- Specialized support groups–You could provide specialized support groups for personal issues such as divorce recovery, grief, abuse recovery; or you could provide 12-Step support groups for addictions such as chemical dependency, codependency, or eating disorders.
- Discipleship group–Members could move to a discipleship course such as *Experiencing God*, *Disciple's Prayer Life*, or *MasterLife*.
- Leader training group–Some selected members could move into a leader training track beginning with a course like *WiseCounsel: Skills for Lay Counseling*.

Goals for a Face-to-Face Support Group

Goals of a Face-to-Face Support Group:

* to help group members identify and understand problems and feelings from childhood experiences;
* to help group members identify ways the past affects them in the present;
* to help group members understand that other people have experienced similar problems and feelings;
* to help group members unlock buried feelings from the past and experience healing and forgiveness;
* to help group members experience an atmosphere of trust, honesty, and unconditional love;
* to help group members identify and remove emotional, psychological, and spiritual barriers to fellowship with God;
* to help group members experience a sense of hope and healing.

✴ To Help Group Members Identify and Understand Problems and Feelings from Childhood Experiences

Children who grow up in dysfunctional families experience emotional pain. The pain may be so intense and so continual that the child learns to shut down certain feelings.

The adult child may be surprised at the suggestion that he is out of touch with his feelings. Face-to-Face Support Groups are designed to help the adult child realize that he may have shut down his emotions and to help him get back in touch with buried feelings.

The group aims to help each person get to the point that he can say, "This is what I am feeling, and this is why I am feeling this way."

✴ To Help Group Members Identify Ways the Past Affects Them in the Present

Members of dysfunctional families practice denial. Denying obvious family and emotional issues becomes a major trait of the family's approach to reality. This pattern of denial may lead an individual to deny that his painful past existed or that it affected him in any significant way. I have shared my story of growing up with an alcoholic father with individuals who responded by saying, "I grew up in an alcoholic family too, but it really didn't affect me." Frequently, such a response is a warning that this individual is denying the significant impact of his childhood experiences.

Face-to-Face Support Groups help group members discover connections between past pain and present behavior. For example, an adult child often learns that he has been influenced heavily by a sense of shame that originated in his family of origin.

✴ To Help Group Members Understand That Other People Have Experienced Similar Problems and Feelings

Children in severely dysfunctional families learn to keep quiet about the family problem. That problem may be alcoholism, abuse, sex addiction, or another form of compulsive behavior. A major rule in dysfunctional families is "Don't talk about the problem." Since the child does not talk about the problem, he is isolated from others who face similar problems. A child of a rageaholic may sit next to another child of a rageaholic in school every day. Neither talks about what is hurting him most. Each could help the other simply by letting him know, "You are not alone." But they have learned the rule of silence, and they honor it. Neither ever learns about the problems the other faces.

After such a child grows up, he may have a vague idea that other people lived in family situations remotely similar to his, but his family's problem still is a private matter and a source of shame.

In a Face-to-Face Support Group the adult child will hear other group members describe incidents from their childhoods. Sooner or later, one of the stories will be enough like his story for him to understand that he is not alone. This is a powerful discovery.

Upon hearing another group member's account of a painful incident from childhood, an internal light comes on: "My emotional pain is not imaginary! It happened to someone else besides me! I know what that person is talking about! She may understand my struggle. She may understand me when I tell my story."

In this respect the participant in a Face-to-Face Support Group is like a person who sets up a campsite in the middle of a desolate valley. The camper feels quite lonely. As darkness settles, camp fires appear one by one around the valley. The camper discovers that he is not alone. He is surrounded by other campers with whom he can communicate. A major component of the healing precipitated by Face-to-Face Support Groups is the discovery, "I am not alone."

✱ To Help Group Members Unlock Buried Feelings from the Past and Experience Healing and Forgiveness

Children can experience so much emotional pain that they stop feeling certain emotions during or soon after a traumatic event. Unless tender and understanding counsel follows the event, its memory may be permanently buried in the child's subconscious mind. This unremembered event is ever-present and ever-active in affecting the individual's thoughts and behavior. Such buried memories frequently are recovered when people participate in Face-to-Face Support Groups. When such memories are faced and discussed, their destructive power can be defused.

✱ To Help Group Members Experience an Atmosphere of Trust, Honesty, and Unconditional Love

Frequently, a strong feeling of the adult child is "If you knew what kind of family I came from and if you knew what I am feeling inside, you could not accept me. You could not love me."

Face-to-Face Support Groups exist to foster an atmosphere of warmth and trust. Individuals learn that some people and some situations are safe. Some people can listen with love. Group members discover, "Some people can see my painful past and still love me."

✱ To Help Group Members Identify and Remove Emotional, Psychological, and Spiritual Barriers to Fellowship with God

One's view of God largely may be shaped by his parents' personalities. Adult children of dysfunctional families may try very hard to have the right view of God and to do the things God wants them to do, while they still lack a sense of a meaningful relationship with Him.

These individuals may find it hard to accept God's love personally because in their experience a father was more angry than he was loving or a mother was more remote than she was giving. Face-to-Face Support Groups can help adult children distinguish between who a parent was and who God is.

Thought and behavior patterns that have resulted from growing up in a dysfunctional family may affect a believer's day-to-day walk with God. For example, perfectionism can rob a believer from feeling that she has ever done enough in her relationship with God. Face-to-Face Support Groups seek to identify and address dysfunctional behaviors that hinder one's walk with God.

✱ To Help Group Members Experience a Sense of Hope and Healing

Face-to-Face Support Groups do not offer solutions to all of a person's emotional problems. The groups equip members with some basic tools and concepts that can be used for continued growth and healing. Group members will learn the importance of working on dysfunctional family issues not just while the group is in progress but for a lifetime. Individuals can leave the group with a sense of hope for continued growth and healing.

What Makes Face-to-Face Support Groups Work?

Face-to-Face Support Groups—
- help hurting people discover they are not alone;
- teach hurting people that some people can be trusted;
- encourage hurting people to be honest about their feelings;
- help hurting people experience emotions that long have been buried;
- offer opportunities to release repressed anger, pain, and fear;
- help hurting people recognize and process their anger toward God;
- help hurting people discover true spirituality in their walk with Christ.

These results can occur when the group is built on certain basic concepts.

Foundational Concepts for Face-to-Face Support Groups

1. All group members must sign the covenant.
2. You must face the past to overcome it.
3. Feelings can be hard to find.
4. Feedback helps people discover their feelings.
5. Emotional baggage should be unpacked.
6. Group members usually feel worse before they feel better.
7. Boundaries must be established or repaired.
8. Spouses should not be in the same group.
9. Affirmation can change the way people think.
10. Prayer can produce emotional healing.

CONCEPT 1: All Group Members Must Sign the Covenant

Each person who participates in a Face-to-Face Support Group must commit to the agreements that appear in the Group Covenant on page 8 in *Making Peace with Your Past* member book.

Through this covenant participants express their initial commitment to the group. The covenant also lets group members know what they can expect from other group members. It is the cement that binds the group together before members experience the closeness of sharing one another's stories and pain. The covenant sets the stage for the confidentiality that is crucial to the group's success. It also alerts the potential group member that the group requires outside work.

The covenant's last paragraphs may surprise you. If group members are using a prescription drug that alters their feelings, and if they cannot stop using it safely, they should inform the facilitator. They should not violate their doctor's instructions. Some prescription drugs require gradually reducing the dosage. They should follow their physician's advice about this.

Group members are challenged to abstain from any sexual involvement outside marriage. Compulsive sexual behavior can numb feelings.

Remember that Face-to-Face Support Groups are meant to target persons both outside and inside the church. Understand that persons who are from dysfunctional families likely will use various forms of compulsive/addictive behavior to stay out of touch with deep emotions.

Challenging group members to withdraw from compulsive behaviors and to refrain from the use of mood-altering drugs is a way to lead them back toward their feelings. Compulsive/addictive behaviors block the feelings the adult child wants to avoid. Stopping the behaviors that mask the pain makes the pain more intense, but it also exposes the source of the pain so care can be administered.

As you discuss the covenant with prospective members, be sure to encourage them to get their doctors' advice before changing their use of prescription drugs.

Some group members may be so completely under the control of a substance or a compulsion that they find themselves unable to stop, even though they have agreed to do so during the time they are members of this group. In this situation, help this person recognize that he or she needs more help than this particular group can give.

Take this opportunity to refer individuals to a professional treatment program or to a group that specializes in addressing a particular type of addictive behavior (see *WiseCounsel: Skills for Lay Counseling*, pp. 38-46, for help in making an effective referral).

Each person who expresses an interest in the group should be asked to read the covenant. Anyone who is not willing to accept and sign the covenant should not be allowed to participate in the group.

CONCEPT 2: You Must Face the Past to Overcome It

"Isn't it better just to forget the past and move on with life?" A good question! Why dig up pain from the past? Doesn't enough pain exist in the present? Why focus on things that are over and finished?

Unprocessed childhood pain can hold on to you with a snapping-turtle grip. It hides behind denial. It is the dark room at the end of the hall. It is the street down which you don't want to walk. It is the part of yourself you don't want to see.

As long as you run from your childhood pain, it controls you. You may protest that you have moved beyond it but just don't want to talk about it. You may say it's useless to dredge up old issues. Your unwillingness to talk about your childhood pain raises the possibility that it still controls you.

Healing for adult children means facing and walking toward the fear. It is like a child who is trying to go to sleep in a dark room. The child sees an object in the shadows. It looks like a monster. The child feels fear. Only one solution exists. The child must turn on the light and walk toward the object. The child needs to look at the object. He needs to handle it. In doing so, he robs the object of its intense power. He may be frightened by the object again, but now he has learned how to face it. The next time it will be a little easier to turn on the light, walk over to the object, and examine it.

Some well-meaning friends may say to the adult child: "Just trust God, and you will be OK. Read the Bible more. Pray more. Have faith." Such statements prove very frustrating to the adult child who is a believer because they make her feel ashamed. A part of her believes that if she just tried harder, or if she just had more faith, everything would be OK. But another part of the adult child knows that she *has* tried trusting more, praying more, and reading the Bible more. She knows that something inside her is hurting. She has discovered that whatever is causing the hurt also is making it hard for her to pray, to read the Bible, and to trust God.

The adult child who is a believer may resort to cynicism if she does not get help quickly. She needs spiritual and psychological assistance to understand and conquer the power her past has over her. She needs the touch of Christ to experience the grace of God not only in her head but also in her heart and emotions.

CONCEPT 3: Feelings Can Be Hard to Find

Getting in touch with your feelings means becoming sensitive to the emotions you are experiencing while you are experiencing them. This process may be simple for some people, but it can be very difficult for the adult child.

The difficulty adult children have in identifying their feelings can stem from several causes.

The emotional circuit-breaker effect. In the face of childhood traumas the emotional pain may have been too great to handle, and an invisible emotional circuit breaker tripped. A voice inside the child said, *It is easier to live without feeling.* A part of the child retreated into a protective shell, a place of safety from emotional bombardment. Suppressing feelings became a habit.

Now the individual does not even realize that he does not know what he is feeling at a given time. In a group, seeing fear on his face, the facilitator may ask him, "What are you feeling now?" But he answers, "Nothing," and he means it. His strong emotion is visible to everyone in the group except himself.

The group facilitator may then turn to other group members and ask, "Are you detecting any feelings from him?" One by one they answer with comments like, "I see fear in his face" or "I'm detecting some fear in the room." You are then able to say to him: "We sense that you are feeling some fear right now. Can you tell us what the fear is about?"

The group member may continue to deny that he is feeling anything. With the group's help he can eventually begin to let himself feel his emotions. He can begin to talk about the fear inside him, a fear so strong that he does not want to acknowledge it.

Some feelings were not permitted. Another reason that feelings can be hard to find is that dysfunctional families tend to permit the expression of some feelings but not of others. For example, sadness may be OK, but anger is not. Or anger may be OK, while fear is not permissible. The forbidden feelings are carefully weeded out over the years until the adult child seems to operate without them. Actually, the forbidden feelings have simply been buried or transferred to another form of expression.

The impact of denial. Children who are reared in dysfunctional families learn to deny reality.
"What's wrong with Mommy?"
"Nothing, she's resting."
Actually, Mom has passed out because she is drunk, but the family is not allowed to say or admit what really is happening. The child sees that his mother has passed out and knows something is wrong. Strong emotions result: fear, shame, worry. But the child is being told to deny not only an accurate assessment of what is happening but also to deny any emotions.

The child is learning to believe that his perceptions of reality are not reliable. When this kind of experience is repeated hundreds of times, the child learns to deny his own feelings. He becomes unable to discern or trust for himself what is normal.

A sense of impending doom. Dysfunctional families often live with a sense of impending doom. Something bad is going to happen. Maybe it is the fear that Dad is going to gamble away the paycheck again. Perhaps it is the fear that "Mommy will hit me again." This sense of impending doom is ever-present. While the family waits for the next calamity to occur, some pleasant things may happen. These happy events normally would be accompanied by happy feelings, but the child learns that feeling happy is dangerous. Feeling happy makes her vulnerable. She must stay prepared for the next crisis, and being happy interferes with that readiness. So even feelings of happiness must be suppressed in order to feel prepared for the next crisis.

Only one family member gets to hurt. Addictive personalities are self-focused. The idea that each person in the family is allowed to have her own emotional pain is foreign to the dysfunctional family. How can a child's sadness over an argument with her friend compete with Dad's shame over his latest drinking binge? The addictive personality dominates the emotional attention of the family. She may deny her emotions while other family members feel her feelings for her. The child comes to believe, *I don't have a right to my feelings. I can't be happy or even sad for myself until Dad is OK.*

CONCEPT 4: Feedback Helps People Discover Their Feelings

Feedback is an emotional mirror in the group that helps group members get in touch with their feelings. Feedback occurs when I tell you what I see and hear you saying. You may not be aware of the messages your facial expressions and body language communicate. What is obvious to me as I watch and listen may be unknown to you, but I can help you see what I see by giving you feedback.

In a Face-to-Face Support Group members often identify subtle emotional cues in other group members' nonverbal behaviors. Group members will learn this skill from you as you explain it to them and as they see you giving feedback.

In an amazing way group members often identify what another person in the group is feeling even when that person is not able to identify what he is feeling.

Feedback is nonjudgmental. When I give feedback, I am not insisting that what I say is the way things are. I am simply reporting what I see and hear.

Feedback is preceded by a search for subtle cues about what is happening emotionally in the group. Joe swallows hard before he speaks. Is he swallowing a feeling that he does not want to feel or express? Mary becomes silent and still while Sue describes an experience of physical abuse. What emotional buttons are being pushed inside Mary while Sue speaks?

As the group facilitator, you often should ask, "May I give you some feedback?" or "Would you be willing to receive some feedback from the group?" In order to feel safe, the group member for whom feedback is intended needs to have the opportunity to give permission for other group members to give him feedback.

Group members should say, "I am sensing some anger" rather than "You are feeling anger." Ask the person who is the focus of the comments to respond with his reaction to the group's feedback. Remind this group member that it is up to him to determine what he is feeling but that similar feedback from multiple group members merits serious attention.

Through feedback adult children begin to discover what reality is. Childhood reality was too painful. Shutting out reality became a way of coping. This selective screening of reality became a habit. Society helps with this habit by offering multiple alternatives to healthy feedback.

Society's alternatives to feedback.
Dishonest feedback. "Do you mind if I arrive late for our appointment tomorrow?"
"That's fine. When will you get there?"
"I will be 30 minutes late."
"No problem."

The phone conversation ends. The person who received the call storms away, shouting: "Late again! That's the fourth time this week." A common alternative to honest feedback is saying what is outwardly polite to the offending person, then complaining to someone else.

Many relationships are characterized by a steady flow of inaccurate communication. Less-than-honest feedback is all too common. When people tell us how they feel about things we say or do, they may or may not be describing what they really feel.

A challenge for your group is to create an atmosphere of honesty and trust from the beginning of the first meeting. As the group facilitator, you will model direct and honest feedback. Feedback should not be brutal or destructive. It should be honest and guided by love.

Malicious feedback. The idea of loving and honest feedback will be a foreign concept for some group members. They may regard words as verbal darts designed to inflict emotional pain. Honest and loving feedback is hard for them to imagine because they have been the victims of a daily stream of unkind words, perhaps from their closest family members. Such persons need time to watch the group process unfold. They need to see loving feedback. Such persons also may need help in learning how to be honest without being brutal.

Socially correct feedback. Another model that may influence group members as they are asked to share feedback with one another is that of saying only what is socially acceptable. Saying the expected, polite thing often means that feedback is inaccurate. Persons who are feeling a strong need to say only what is nice also may attempt to rescue a group member when he or she is receiving feedback from the group. The group facilitator needs to be aware of this and needs to decide either to interrupt the rescue or lovingly to confront the rescuer about his behavior.

Examples of healthy feedback.
- "I see a lot of pain on your face."
- "You are sitting in a slumped position. Your body seems to be telling us that you are depressed."
- "I felt a lot of fear as I heard you tell that story."
- "What you just shared took a lot of courage. I am proud of you for sharing it."
- "You said that your anger focused on your father. I also heard you expressing a lot of anger toward your mother."
- "What you said helped me get in touch with some pain about my childhood. Thank you very much for sharing."

Confrontation as a form of feedback. Confrontation is a form of feedback that addresses another person's denial. Confrontation should be neither hostile nor destructive. Many times confrontation can be the key to helping a group member move out of a state of complete denial about his emotional condition.

Here are some examples of confrontational feedback:
- "Even though you have not said anything during the meeting, I am sensing a lot of anger in you."
- "If growing up with an abusive parent did not affect you, why are you so reluctant to talk about it?"
- "I get the feeling that you are not telling us what really is bothering you."

CONCEPT 5: Unpack Emotional Baggage

Repressed anger needs release. A child who is abused or neglected may feel angry. Because it is not safe for someone to have such anger toward an abusive parent, the individual must bury or repress such anger in some other way.

Unexpressed anger is like steam under pressure. The unexpressed anger exerts constant pressure on an individual. The pressure may be felt as depression. It may express itself as a physical problem, such as a headache, or in other ways. Individuals need to identify and release such anger.

Quiet people can be very angry. Adult children who are extremely nice and polite frequently are very angry individuals. These people learned to cope with dysfunctional families by becoming people pleasers, by always doing the right things even when they were hurting terribly inside. "Don't rock the boat" became their motto. "I'll be nice, and you'll leave me alone."

People frequently nest such anger below a layer of fear which lingers from childhood terror of a family life that was out of control. The inner self of such an adult thinks that it is still a child in danger, unsafe and unprotected.

Processing anger. In the group process members seek to make contact with the fear, then dig below the fear for the anger it hides. The anger needs to be released in a way that does not harm anyone. Sometimes this will be accomplished simply by talking about the anger.

Fears must be faced. When a family is out of control because of a parent's unpredictable addictive/compulsive behavior, life looks frightening to the child. A child may respond by acting afraid of nothing, or he may be afraid of everything. As an adult, he may fear failure because he experienced conditional love. He may fear success because success seems foreign to what he experienced as a child or because he has learned to believe that the good always precedes the bad.

The adult child must take the courageous step of walking toward his fear. By facing his fear in a group of caring fellow strugglers and with God's help, he can overcome it. He can recognize that God's help makes him stronger than the things he fears.

Shame must be given back. Adult children of dysfunctional families learn to carry other people's shame. Addictive personalities refuse to own their own feelings. Feelings of shame float freely in the dysfunctional family until another family member catches them.

A child of a sex addict learns to feel shame for the parent's behavior. It's as if the child himself is the sex addict. This shame coats the whole life of the child. He learns to feel shame for things that merit no shame. He learns to feel shame simply for having feelings. Finally, he learns to feel shame for existing. He becomes a shame magnet. It is as though he begins attracting shame all around.

The adult child must learn to give back the shame emotionally to the responsible person. At the same time, an adult child must confess, repent, and find cleansing for any shameful behavior that is his responsibility.

CONCEPT 6: Group Members Usually Feel Worse Before They Feel Better

The reason is simple. If members have not been in touch with buried feelings of pain, anger, shame, and fear, and through the group process they begin to feel some of these long-buried feelings, they will feel worse initially. But as the feelings are experienced and discussed, a cleansing occurs that frees members to go on with life. Then things start to get better.

Group members may be surprised by the intensity of the downward spiral of emotions that can occur for the first four to six weeks of the group. Group members often feel excited and happy because they finally have found a way to deal with pain from the past, at the same time feeling the sadness accompanying the discovery of the loss and pain they long have denied.

If this is the first time your church has provided support groups, you must help the group through this difficult time. If the group does not move on to the healing process, your church's whole support-group ministry could be aborted due to a lack of understanding about support groups.

CONCEPT 7: Boundaries Must Be Established or Repaired

Boundaries are protective barriers that give us control over how we live our lives and how other people relate to us. If someone tries to force sexual involvement on me, I have the right to say no. That is a boundary.

Boundaries are not the same as walls. Walls shut out people and feelings. Walls keep me isolated from reality. Boundaries are flexible, depending on the situation and the persons involved. Boundaries are like filters. I let some things in. I keep some things out. I decide who gets close and who does not.

People who as children experience abuse have broken boundaries. A child who is sexually abused may grow up thinking that he or she does not have the right to say no to someone's sexual advance. A child who grows up being abused physically may believe that he does not have the right to stop someone from hurting him. A child who experiences verbal abuse may decide that it is normal to have people yelling at him or belittling him on a daily basis. These all are broken boundaries.

Adult children can build new boundaries in their lives. Walls can be removed. Damaged boundaries can be repaired.

Emotional boundaries. Emotional boundaries protect against verbal abuse. Emotional boundaries set limits on manipulative behavior by others. Emotional boundaries remind me that I can feel my own feelings. I am not bound to feel the feelings of other people for them.

Physical boundaries. Physical boundaries include signals about where and when I will permit a particular person to touch me. Physical boundaries concern my right to protect myself from physical harm.

Sexual boundaries. Sexual boundaries mean that I can say no to sexual advances. I have the right to set limits on what others do to me sexually. This may seem obvious to most people, but it may not be obvious to the victim of sexual abuse.

Spiritual boundaries. A healthy relationship with Jesus Christ is the only form of true religion. Religion, including some distorted expressions of the Christian faith, can be used to manipulate and control through fear, shame, and guilt.

Spiritual boundaries mean that I can make choices about my commitment to Christ. I do not have to be manipulated by persons who seek to control my feelings and my life with twisted versions of religious truth. I can say no to people who attempt to portray God as unloving and unforgiving.

Damage to one type of boundary often can spill over and affect a person's ability to establish healthy boundaries in other areas. Many adult children need healing for the whole range of boundaries. Working on just one set often is not sufficient.

CONCEPT 8: Spouses Should Not Be in the Same Group

Adult children tend to marry other adult children and form codependent marriages. Adult children of dysfunctional families often live out a compulsion to rescue other people. A characteristic of codependency is taking care of other people in inappropriate ways.

If a husband and a wife participate in the same support group, several dangers are present.
- One of the two might not feel comfortable talking about his or her feelings and experiences in front of the other one.
- One spouse might be tempted to reinterpret the other's comments and feelings for the group. This would handicap the group process.
- When the group confronts one spouse, the other spouse might try to defend him or her, thus interrupting the group process.

Some alternatives would be for one spouse to go through a group. The other partner then would participate in the next group offered. Another suggestion is that each spouse could be in a different group if two groups were offered simultaneously.

In some cases the same dangers apply to two close friends. The two could be emotionally enmeshed to an extent that it would be impossible for them both to participate effectively in the same group.

CONCEPT 9: Affirmation Can Change the Way People Think

Growing up in a dysfunctional family can mean suffering a constant barrage of negative messages. Some of the messages are spoken. Others are nonverbal. These messages are heard so frequently that they become like a tape that plays over and over inside one's head.

Part of the healing process in a Face-to-Face Support Group is the use of daily affirmation. An affirmation is a positive statement designed to replace the negative tapes in your head. Each unit has a different affirmation associated with its topic. A new affirmation will be added each week. Group members are asked to say aloud the affirmations each day.

Consider having the group say the affirmations together as part of some sessions.

Here is a list of the affirmations.
- I accept God's love for me.
- God is in control.
- Through Jesus Christ I am clean in God's sight.
- I release my fears to Jesus.
- I claim the joy of being God's child.
- Because God loves me, it is OK to be incomplete.
- I accept God's healing of the painful memories of my past.
- No matter what happens, I trust that God is working for my good.
- In Christ it is OK for me to be myself.
- Because God has forgiven me, I can forgive others.
- I am blessed.

Another affirmation used in the Face-to-Face Support Group is the phrase "I support you." Use the phrase "I support you" to encourage a group member when he gets stuck emotionally and after someone has shared something painful. Teach the members of your group to use the phrase. When the group is functioning well, members will use the phrase spontaneously at different times throughout the meeting.

CONCEPT 10: Prayer Can Produce Emotional Healing

One daily assignment asks group members to pray for one another by name each day.

As the group facilitator, give special attention to praying for specific needs of the members of your group. This will mean a lot to your group members. Each session will close with prayer. The closing prayer time, though brief, can be powerful.

You may choose to utilize prayer at other times in the group. Be careful not to use prayer as a substitute for talking through an emotional issue that needs to be discussed. Be open to using prayer as a tool for emotional healing.

Your great weakness as a facilitator may be the times in which you don't know what to do. At those times ask the group to join you in seeking God's direction. Help members learn a practical dependence on their Heavenly Father.

After you have given appropriate opportunities for emotional release, a focused prayer for an individual can be a powerful tool. You may want to ask the group member to sit in the center of the circle while other group members touch him or her. (Group members should get permission before touching the person during the prayer time.) Invite volunteers to pray simple prayers of petition and affirmation for the person in the center of the circle. This type of prayer is a powerful expression of support by the group as well as an effective way of lifting up his or her needs to God.

Regularly pray for each person in your group. Send notes of encouragement on occasion.

Recommended Reading for Understanding Issues

- *Caring Enough to Confront*, rev. ed. David Augsburger (Ventura, CA: GL Regal Books, 1980).
- *Untangling Relationships*: *A Christian Perspective on Codependency*, Pat Springle. (Houston, TX: Rapha Publishing 1993).
- *Getting Unstuck*, Pat Springle. (Houston and Dallas, TX: Rapha Publishing/Word, Inc., 1992).
- *Healing for Adult Children of Alcoholics*, Sara Hines Martin. (Nashville: Broadman Press, 1991).
- *Healing of Memories*, David A. Seamands. (Wheaton: Victor Books, 1985).
- *Intimacy: The Longing of Every Human Heart*, Terry Hershey. (Eugene, Oregon: Harvest House Publishers, 1984).
- *LIFE Support Leader's Handbook*. (Nashville: LifeWay Press, 1993). Available for download at no charge from *http://www.lifeway.com/download.asp*.
- *Love Is a Choice: Recovery for Codependent Relationships*, Robert Hemfelt, Frank Minirth, and Paul Meier. (Nashville: Thomas Nelson Publishers, 1989).
- *Meeting Needs Through Support Groups*, Sara Hines Martin. (Birmingham: New Hope, 1992).
- *Search for Significance* LIFE® Support Group Series Edition, Robert S. McGee. (Houston: Rapha Publishing, 1992).
- *Shame on You!* Sara Hines Martin. (Nashville: Broadman Press, 1991).
- *The Blessing*, Gary Smalley and John Trent. (Nashville: Thomas Nelson Publishers, 1990).
- *The Dangers of Growing Up in a Christian Home*, Donald E. Sloat. (Nashville: Thomas Nelson Publishers, 1986).

Basic Skills for Group Leadership

This section discusses basic skills needed to lead a Face-to-Face Support Group. Each week you will be asked to work on some of the specific skills described in this section.

* Be personally involved without relinquishing leadership.
* Be willing to confront in love.
* Communicate acceptance and concern.
* Create a feeling of safety in the group.
* Facilitate feedback.
* Guide the expression of anger.
* Help group members connect the past with the present.
* Help group members identify their feelings.
* Integrate biblical and psychological truth.
* Operate the group on a feeling level.
* Know how to start a session.
* Know how to end a session.
* Keep one person from dominating the group.
* Read nonverbal communication.
* Utilize good listening skills.
* Stay ready for anything.
* Teach group members to help one another.
* Validate feelings.

* Be Personally Involved Without Relinquishing Leadership

Your role as group facilitator is not that of a trained expert who has solved all his problems and who shows up each week to help struggling group members with their problems. Your role is that of a fellow struggler. You are a leader who also understands the emotional pain of others.

You need to be emotionally vulnerable. Sharing some of your own emotional pain is crucial. However, also recognize that someone needs to be leading the group at all times. This means that you may not be able to move as deeply into personal sharing as a group member can. You should be involved, but do not dominate the group session.

From the first session, perhaps even during the preliminary interviews with prospective group members, you will set the tone for the group sessions. If you model openness about your own struggles, the group will follow that example. If you display a condescending attitude, group members will find it hard to trust you or each other and to share with you or with each other in the sessions.

Never attempt to create emotions you don't feel. Never try to magnify your emotions to be a good example. The keys are letting yourself get in touch with your feelings and then being honest about these feelings.

* Be Willing to Confront in Love

Sometimes love is tough. Sometimes caring for a person means being willing to say something to that person that he or she does not want to hear. The prevalence of denial in the lives of adult children ensures that some confrontation will be necessary in your group.

Confrontation, motivated by love, is sensitive to timing and wording. It is not hostile or destructive. It is sensitive to how much the recipient can handle at the time of the confrontation.

If you feel that every conflict must be smoothed over or ignored, you will have trouble leading this group. Conflict is not always bad. Confrontation can lead to understanding and healing.

* Communicate Acceptance and Concern

Shame is a significant issue for adult children. Adult children carry shame for a parent's behavior and also for their own behavior. Adult children often feel that they have something to hide. In this group you want to create an atmosphere that feels safe. You want to create an atmosphere that communicates, "I accept you as you are."

Accepting a person as he is does not necessarily mean that you agree with the person's values or choices. You can love a person without agreeing with the person. If a person's values need to change, those values are more likely to be influenced by a caring, sympathetic friend than by a judgmental critic.

In the group you will hear members tell about things that make them ashamed. Sometimes the shame is irrational. It is about what someone else did, not about what the member did. Sometimes the shame will be appropriate. In either case your role is not to make moral pronouncements but to relate to this person in love.

How do you communicate acceptance and concern? Here are some simple guidelines.

- Listen intently and aggressively.
- When someone shares something emotionally painful, lean toward her. Use facial expressions to show concern. Nod your head. When the person has to stop because the emotion is too strong, say, "I support you."
- When a group member cries and says, "I'm sorry," say: "It's OK to cry in this group. We are here to share your pain."
- Resist the temptation to make moral judgments every time a group member describes a situation you believe to be wrong. This could make the group member feel that it would not be safe to share again.
- The first priority of this group is helping the group member get in touch with her feelings. As you build a relationship with the person, you will have significant opportunities to influence moral choices later in the relationship. Do not interpret this stance as a lack of concern for moral values. It is a matter of strategy, of how you can get to the point of having a significant impact on this person's life.
- After a group member has shared something that makes him feel vulnerable and ashamed, say something like: "I know that sharing what you just shared took a lot of courage. I admire you for being able to share it."
- If a group member condemns the actions of another group member who has shared, quickly intervene. Remind members that they are not in the group to judge one another.

✴ Create a Feeling of Safety in the Group

Adult children need a safe place emotionally. Some participants in your group may feel that they have never had such a place. They may be skeptical of the idea that such a place exists. Part of your role as the group facilitator is to help create an atmosphere of safety and trust in the group. Here are some ways you can accomplish this goal.

Confidentiality. During the first session and during several subsequent sessions remind the group how important confidentiality is. Kindly but firmly remind the group that anyone who breaks the commitment to confidentiality will be asked to leave the group. Reaffirm your commitment to confidentiality.

Remind the group that even telling someone else's story without using names violates a confidence. You inadvertently may share with the one person who can put the pieces together.

When you discuss the covenant with prospective group members, you may want to reserve the right to confer with a professional counselor or with another adviser on issues that come up in the group. Make this clear before the group starts.

Confidence. As you lead the group, at times you will feel that you do not know what you are doing. At those times lean on God's direction and follow the instincts He gives you. You will make mistakes. The best facilitators do.

Be honest about your personal struggles and be open to the comments that group members make about your leadership. At the same time, starting with the first contacts you have with group members, you should convey an attitude of confidence. Your attitude and words should communicate: "This group is going to be a positive experience. It is going to provide a lot of help to the persons who participate in it. I feel that God has called me to lead this group, and it will work!"

Learn to distinguish the difference between openness, vulnerability, and humility on one hand and a lack of self-confidence as a facilitator on the other hand. You want the former, not the latter.

Privacy. The group needs a sense of privacy about what it is doing. This starts with your choice of an appropriate meeting place. It is affected by how you deal with persons who might mistakenly open the door during a session. It is affected by how you talk about the group in public.

Group members must sense that you are committed to keeping private what happens in the group. You will not earn their trust if you are unable to communicate this commitment.

Boundaries. As the group facilitator, you will enforce certain boundaries during the sessions. You will not permit a group member to abuse another group member verbally. You will not force group members to do or say anything unwillingly. You will recognize the difference between gently pushing a group member to a point of discovery and growth and manipulative force, which pushes the individual to behavior that is against his will.

Christian identity. Many persons in your group will come because it is a Christian group sponsored by a church. They need to hear you make a clear connection between what the group is doing and your personal faith in Christ. They may fear that what they are doing somehow violates their faith. They may have heard that all recovery work is associated with the New Age movement or with secular psychology. All that is done in the group should honor Christ and His Word. Let group members know where you stand by being open about your commitment to Christ and to His Word.

✴ Facilitate Feedback

Your members can learn to give feedback. After you have explained and modeled the concept, consciously wait long enough for other group members to give feedback. Let them learn that you will not always be the first one to speak.

Watch the faces of group members as they listen to someone share. If you see anyone exhibit strong emotion in facial expressions or other body language, ask that person if he is willing to give feedback. Here's how the process can work.

With little emotion, Jane tells a story of sexual abuse. She tells it almost as if she were an uninvolved observer. As you look at the members of the group who are listening to Jane, you sense anger in them. They are angry with the perpetrator of the abuse. But Jane, who should be the most angry, does not appear to be. You see a different response in one group member, Donna, whose face reveals terror.

Jane reaches a stopping point in her story. You turn to Linda and ask, "What were you feeling while Jane talked?" Linda responds: "I was very angry with her father. Jane did not deserve to be treated like that." You can detect a bit of anger in Linda's voice as she speaks. You turn to another group member and ask, "What did you feel?" "I felt anger, too. I wanted to hurt her father."

As Jane listens to this, she is somewhat surprised. Does this mean that she had a right to be angry about what happened to her? At this point Jane actually may take the first step toward getting in touch with the anger she felt. The anger felt by the other group members becomes an emotional mirror in which she can see herself.

Now you turn to Donna. "Donna, what were you feeling when Jane was speaking?" Donna doesn't want to respond. She has moved into an almost unmanageable level of fear , and she fears that she may lose control.

You press gently but directly for a response: "Donna, I am sensing a lot of fear in you right now. What is that fear about?"
"I don't know," she replies.

"Are you feeling fear?"
"Yes, a lot of fear."
"Donna, what is this fear about? Why did Jane's story make you so afraid?"
"I don't know."
"Donna, when was the first time you can remember feeling fear like this?"

As Donna responds to your questions, you may help her uncover a forgotten but powerful incident of abuse in her past. After taking some time to respond to Donna, you would want to return to Jane to help her process what she has said. Always attempt to return to the original group member who shared so she has closure and does not feel neglected.

This example illustrates the two-way nature of feedback. Feedback helps a group member see what other group members see in him. And feedback can shift the focus to another group member who discovered something emotionally intense by listening to someone else tell his story.

✴ Guide the Expression of Anger

One of your goals is to help group members get in touch with their anger. When a group member gets in touch with his anger, he needs a way to express it. Part of your role is to make certain anger is expressed constructively.

Anger that results in physical harm to the individual, to another group member, or to the room in which you are meeting is not acceptable. Anger toward a parent that is redirected toward a group member or toward you as the group facilitator must be confronted.

You need not make moral pronouncements about a group member's anger if it is aimed in the wrong direction. Your job is to help channel the anger in the right direction.

Often the fact that someone is able to get in touch with any anger at all is an accomplishment. Rather than squelching the anger, try to redirect it.

In one session a woman named Marty was talking about her struggle to decide whether to leave her husband. While Marty was speaking, another woman in the group, Leslie, jumped up and moved quickly toward the door.

As she was walking out the door, she said in a voice full of anger and frustration: "I'm sorry, but I must leave. What she is doing is wrong."

I asked Leslie if she would sit down for a minute before she left the group. I feared that if she left, she never would come back to another session. I was surprised at her anger. She had appeared quiet and controlled. She agreed to sit down but not in the group circle. She sat down in a chair about 10 feet from where the group was sitting.

I talked to Leslie about what she was feeling. She indicated that she was extremely angry with Marty. In fact, she was furious with Marty. This seemed strange because the group had been meeting for only a short time, and Leslie did not know Marty well.

I asked her questions like "Why do you think Marty's comments are making you so angry?" We continued to talk, and soon I persuaded her to come and sit inside the circle again. When she returned, Marty began trying to defend the comments she had made earlier. I said: "Marty, I don't think this anger is about you. I think it is about something else." I asked her to stop defending her comments.

I began to ask Leslie where she thought this tremendous anger was coming from. I showed her that because the extreme intensity of her anger toward Marty did not make sense, it must be coming from somewhere else. Through a series of probing questions I discovered that Leslie's mother had left home when Leslie was about 12.

That night for the first time Leslie admitted that the word *abandoned* described how she felt. She discovered that the intense anger she was feeling was not really toward Marty but toward her mother. By talking about the anger, by talking about how it felt for her mother to leave when she was a young girl, Leslie found the starting point for moving beyond the pain of abandonment.

Marty actually had helped Leslie. As a child, Leslie could not permit herself to feel the intense anger evoked by her mother's behavior. The anger had been locked away. As Marty spoke, Leslie felt that she was looking in on her mother as she made the decision that would leave her alone. Leslie felt that she could not be angry with her mother, but she could be angry with Marty, whom she hardly knew. Leslie had previously followed a pattern of running away from emotionally intense situations. She had tried to run away this time, but her group had lovingly pulled her back to confront her pain.

This incident illustrates that misdirected anger can be harnessed as a tool to get to the root of a buried problem. A good step in early stages is to encourage the person to say, "I feel angry" or "I feel very angry with _____ because _____ . Help the angry member move beyond the anger to forgiveness. Progress probably will take time and much prayer.

✴ Help Group Members Connect Past, Present

Pain from the past affects present behavior. Sharpen your ability to see connections. Watch for things that don't add up. Detect feelings. Ask probing questions.

Suppose a group member identifies a feeling of fear. Ask, "Can you remember a time in your childhood when you felt this same feeling?" or "Can you remember the first time you felt this particular kind of fear?" Then ask, "What happened to make you feel this way when you were a child?"

Often you will uncover an incident from childhood that is having a powerful impact on this person's present life. Help the group member see connections between past pain and present issues. Offer insights.

For example, a member of your group describes an extraordinary fear of walking into a new group of people. In many ways this person is competent and confident, but he has a sense of inferiority that seems out of proportion to any weaknesses you can observe.

As you watch and listen, you sense that this person is operating from a shame-based identity. You will want to help this person make the connection between shame from the past and fear of people in the present.

You could probe to find incidents from childhood that led to a feeling of shame. To provide clues about how shame originated in his life, you could ask questions about how his parents regarded him.

After you discover sources of the shame, you could explain some of the ways shame from the past affects the way we relate to people in the present. You could also encourage this person to call shame by its name anytime he feels it. Identifying shame and remembering its source are the first steps toward overcoming it.

✴ Help Group Members Identify Feelings

To help group members identify their feelings, you will focus on a narrow range of feelings, using this list: anger, fear, guilt, joy, loneliness, shame, peace, hope.

Although this list is limited, it includes the feelings with which adult children are most likely to have problems.

During group sessions you frequently will ask group members, "What are you feeling? Anger? Fear? Guilt? Joy? Loneliness? Sadness? Shame?" Challenge group members to identify with one of these feelings. Often a group member will respond that he does not know what he is feeling or that he is not feeling anything. He probably is telling the truth, having had a lifetime of practice in avoiding his feelings. By asking the question repeatedly, you can teach this person to probe his feelings, to discover them, and to call them by name.

Sometimes you will look at a group member's face and detect that he is afraid. You will then ask, "What are you feeling?" He may respond, "I don't know." You will reply, "Could we get some feedback from the group?" If he answers yes, one by one three different group members say something like "I see fear in your face" or "I detect some fear." You will encourage the group member to accept this feedback. He then can say to himself, *They are telling me that I appear to feel fear.* He then can decide whether he is actually feeling fear and can begin the process of learning to identify fear when he experiences it.

On other occasions a group member wil begin to get in touch with a feeling but then bury it. You may observe this happening when the person takes a deep breath, holds it for a second, and then releases it. Or it may be done with a gulp—*swallowing a feeling.* When this happens, you may ask: "What were you feeling just now when you swallowed hard? You looked as if you were in pain before you swallowed, but now you appear to feel nothing." The group member will be surprised and probably does not even realize what happened. Your comments can help her identify the feeling. A good follow-up question would be "Why did you need to run away from that feeling?" or "Do you always bury that particular feeling when you have it?" or "Do you bury all intense feelings?" or "Where did you learn to stuff feelings inside rather than feel them?"

When the group disbands, each group member should have become more sensitive to the presence and identity of his or her emotions at any given time.

✱ Integrate Biblical and Psychological Truth

Making Peace with Your Past is built on biblical and psychological truth. As you lead the group, encourage a healthy balance of biblical and psychological input. Biblical truth and true psychology do not conflict with each other. Psychological insights should support biblical truth. Religious phrases should not be used as tools for denying emotional problems. Help group members come to a psychological understanding of themselves in the context of biblical truth.

The idea is not that each session should have a psychological/emotional segment and a separate spiritual segment. Lead group members to examine childhood issues through the dual lenses of theology and psychology.

Be careful about using statements like "God is telling me to tell you …" Assume that if God is leading you, the recipients of your message will sense God's presence in what you say.

✱ Operate the Group on a Feeling Level

Some group members will resist getting in touch with feelings. You may remark to a group member that you sense a lot of shame behind some of his comments, and he may respond, "Yes, I read a good book on shame" and then proceed to give a logical commentary on the topic of shame. Confront such a person with comments like "I'm glad that you read a good book on shame, but I want to know what you are feeling. I sense that you are feeling shame. Let's talk about your shame."

Sometimes the whole group will gravitate toward a logical discussion to avoid getting in contact with feelings. Your role should always be to pull the group back to the feeling level. Frequently, you will need to ask several group members, "What are you feeling right now?" When a member answers with something like "I am feeling some sadness," respond by asking, "What is this sadness about?" or "What does this sadness feel like?" or "Where does this sadness come from?"

Don't be afraid of silence. Learn to hear feelings in the group even when verbal silence exists. Be patient. Let the group members make their own discoveries.

Take the time necessary to probe and explore. Remember, you are not in the group to dispense crisp, logical answers to every problem or to quote a Bible verse and expect the hurt to disappear instantly. Be sensitive to your own reactions to feelings in the group. If you feel fear in the room, you may need to say: "I am feeling fear right now. Is anyone else feeling fear?" Let the group members respond.

Powerful expressions of emotion may occur in your group. When someone begins to cry, give him time to cry. Do not change the subject. Do not turn the discussion to another group member. Do not say, "It's OK; don't cry." Let the person cry for a while. Use statements like "It's OK to cry." "It's OK to feel your emotions." "This is a safe place to cry."

Observe how other group members react to this person's crying. Some obviously will feel their own emotions. Others may appear detached. These responses can be revealing.

When a group member obviously is detached, while others in the group are very emotionally involved, you can ask him, "What are you feeling?" The person may seem perplexed by his inability to name a feeling. He has shut down emotionally. This response may feel so normal for him that he does not realize that he is out of sync with the group's feeling level.

Ask, "Do you think it is unusual that while everyone else in the group is deeply involved emotionally, you are not?" Through this process you may help a group member identify the fact that he has denied basic emotional responses.

A key element in keeping the group on a feeling level is your willingness to stay in touch with your own feelings. If you refuse to allow yourself to feel your emotions, the group will follow your lead. Do not be afraid to say at various points in the session, "I am feeling some sadness" or "I am feeling some fear right now."

✷ Know How to Start a Session

Arrive at the meeting place early. Greet group members as they arrive. Attempt to detect any feelings in group members as they arrive. Start the session when it is scheduled to start. Begin by inviting group members to check in. Checking in means giving a brief report, which could focus on any one of several areas.

Start the check-in time by asking, "Does anyone have anything pressing that you need to share today?" or "What happened in your life this past week as a result of our previous session?" Intense issues may have been raised by the study material for the week or by something that happened during or since the previous group session. A group member may need to talk about such an issue as soon as the group begins. Be willing to respond to any pressing issue that is raised during the initial period of checking in.

✷ Know How to End a Session

You face two dangers in ending a session. One is ending the session at a specific time in response to a rigid schedule. If you operate this way, you may end at a point when a group member finally is in touch with a significant emotion and is ready to share. The group

member will not necessarily be at the same point of readiness when you start the next session.

The other danger is that if you continue the session too long, some group members will become tired and frustrated. Spouses of group members may worry and begin to develop negative feelings about the group.

Make every effort to end at the planned time. Invite members to stay and talk with you if they feel the need. Learn to be flexible about when to end the session, but do not consistently end it later than the target time for adjourning. If a meeting runs over, you may need to give permission for persons to leave if they must.

About 30 minutes before you are ready to close the session, lead the person on whom you are focusing to a point of closure. Then ask, "Does anyone else have anything you need to talk about?" Take some time to respond to issues that are raised. At some point cut off the discussion.

Affirm the importance of what is being said. Offer to begin the next session with that topic. Plan to ask the group member on whom you focused last to introduce the topic if he feels the need to discuss it further.

Before adjourning, be sure you have tied up loose ends.
- Did you put someone on hold during the session? Did you ever get back to him?
- Was someone's sharing interrupted when you shifted the focus to someone's response?
- Did you reach closure with the original speaker?

Finally, ask group members to stand and join hands. Encourage group members to say sentence prayers on "something that happened in this session that I am thankful for" or "a problem I am working on." Invite each person to pray only for himself or herself during the prayer.

Some group members may hesitate to pray aloud. State that if anyone does not want to pray aloud, he should simply say "Amen" when it is his turn to pray. Don't make this too easy. The prayer time at the end is an important tool that allows group members to make positive statements about progress in the session.

Prayer also has intrinsic value as people respond to God. Sometimes this guide will make specific suggestions for the closing prayer.

After the closing prayer the session is over. Do not allow the discussion of issues after the closing prayer.

✷ Keep One Person from Dominating

A characteristic of the Face-to-Face Support Group is that each person has an opportunity to talk. While avoiding any sense of hurry, be aware that some members will talk too long. When a person is going into too much detail and is losing the group's attention, you need to get things back on course. When this occurs, you usually will notice that the person sharing is dealing with facts more than feelings. You will need to shift the group back to a feeling level.

Discreetly interrupt the person who has talked too long. One way is to interrupt and restate what you have heard: "So what you are saying is. . . ." Another way is to interrupt and restate your original question: "What is causing you to feel shame?" The speaker may be somewhat unsettled by this response but should respond by restating the response more succinctly. Another method is to interrupt and ask the person if he or she would mind getting feedback from the group.

✷ Read Nonverbal Communication

As the group facilitator, become a student of nonverbal communication. Much of what happens to group members as they respond to the content of the session first will be expressed nonverbally. Sometimes the nonverbal cue will communicate a terribly important message. Here are some signs to look for.

Posture and body orientation. How is an individual sitting in relation to the rest of the group? Is he turning outward as if he would like to face the other way? Is she leaning forward and listening intently, communicating interest and involvement?

Facial signals. Learn to read faces. Scan the group while a member shares a painful childhood incident. Look for signs of intense emotional involvement. Depend on God for sensitivity. Is anyone's face full of pain? Is someone holding back tears? What messages are conveyed by each group member's face? Do you detect fear? Do you sense the person is in intense thought? Does it appear that this individual has shut down all emotions?

Breathing patterns, gulps, sighs. Listen for sighs, deep breaths, gulps, and so forth. Notice the timing of these responses. What do they mean? Ask questions.

✷ Utilize Good Listening Skills
Another aspect of your leadership role is aggressive listening. Much will consist of visual listening, watching for nonverbal cues. Listen carefully and store what you

hear. Consider making notes after each session to help you remember what various group members shared. Some may most effectively a group member when you can provide help to relate something he just said to something he said a few weeks ago.

Here are some listening tips:

- When one group member is speaking, visually scan the other group members occasionally. What are they saying nonverbally?
- Remember occasionally to restate and summarize what a group member has just said to the group. Then ask, "Is that what you said?" Let the group member respond.
- Remember to face the person who is speaking and to lean toward the speaker.
- When appropriate, nod your head to show that you are hearing what someone is saying. Use an occasional verbal phrase to indicate that you are listening to what someone is saying.
- When necessary, stop the speaker and ask for clarification of what was just said.
- Make sure that someone in the group gives a response when a person says something that needs a response.

✷ Stay Ready for Anything

Don't try to predict or anticipate everything that will happen in a group session. Some of the most significant occurrences will not be planned and may not clearly related to your agenda or to the topic for the week. If you are a person who needs to have everything planned, you will have to work on being spontaneous during the group sessions. Not knowing what will happen can produce fear. Lean on God. Trust Him to help you, no matter what happens. See the specific helps in "Dealing with Problems," page 26.

✷ Teach Group Members to Help One Another

As the group progresses, you will encourage group members to do more and more of the work in helping one another. You will model certain ways of responding and relating. After a few sessions you should not be the only one asking questions like, "What are you feeling right now?" or "I support you." Other group members should volunteer insights after listening to a person share. As the group catches on to these concepts, you may find yourself saying less and less.

✱ Validate Feelings

Remember that sharing emotions will be hard for some members of your group. When a group member shares an emotion, commend him for sharing. Use statements like "I know it must have been hard for you to share that just then. Thank you for exercising the courage to share." Jim may weep convulsively and then apologize. A good response would be to ask several group members: "How do you feel about Jim's crying? Does it make you respect him less?" You will know which group members to ask, and you can expect them to respond with words like "I admire someone who can let his emotions out. I support Jim for being able to cry. I think he did the right thing."

Adult children need to get in touch with buried anger they feel toward parents or significant other people in their lives. Help them to see that pretending that the feeling does not exist accomplishes nothing. The feeling needs to be experienced, acknowledged, then dealt with. The ultimate goal is not to create anger toward their parents. The goal is to process anger that is present but hidden, then to move on to healing.

Avoid telling a person that he is feeling the wrong thing or that he is wrong for having a certain feeling. Your group will include persons who have trouble even finding their feelings. Once they find a feeling, they will need help learning how to name the feeling and deciding how to respond. After they develop these skills, they will be ready to learn more about how to relate to people in a way that makes it less likely they will experience destructive feelings.

Additional Leadership Helps

✱ Visiting Other Support Groups for Insights

Visiting a support group may help as you prepare to lead a Face-to-Face Support Group, although you may not agree with everything you see and hear there. You may observe some ideas that will help you. Check with neighboring churches to see if they have open support groups that you can attend and observe in action. You also may consider groups like Alcoholics Anonymous, Adult Children of Alcoholics, Overeaters Anonymous, and Codependents Anonymous.

✱ Dealing with Problems

What if someone loses control? Someone in your group may get in touch with emotions so deep that he or she loses control and needs special help. First, decide what you will do before the time comes you need to respond. You may want to carry notes or phone numbers for quick reference.

If you should face such an experience, take steps to protect the individual from harming himself or other people. Do not panic. Decide whether you need to call an ambulance for professional assistance.

Here's how one group responded to an unexpected event in a Face-to-Face Support Group session. While a group member was sharing, a man in the group suddenly jumped up and kicked a chair several feet

across the room. Then he let out an agonizing cry and left the room. Next we heard a loud noise, which we soon discovered was the sound of this large man's fist being driven through a hallway wall.

At first we were so shocked that we sat there frozen. After a few seconds the whole group ran to the hallway. The man was leaning against the wall, weeping profusely. One by one, group members surrounded him, each touching him in a comforting way. Different persons began to comfort him. After a few minutes the group coaxed him into the room to draw him back into the group process. Something he heard in the session suddenly put him in touch with intense pain from the past. The group's response was a beautiful example of how a group of diverse people can reach out in love.

In this case the group did not need outside help. The group was able to respond to a surprising and, at first, frightening situation. Do not underestimate your group's ability to help a person who is in deep emotional turmoil. At the same time, do not hesitate to call for outside help if necessary.

If you do not know when and how to make referrals for professional help, study pages 38-46 in *WiseCounsel: Skills for Lay Counseling.*

What happens if inappropriate relationships develop? People get close to one another in Face-to-Face Support Groups. The interaction of men and women in the small-group atmosphere of openness and honesty is one key to the group's effectiveness. However, you need to warn group members of the potential danger of emotionally intense male-female relationships. If a group member is in an emotionally damaged marriage, he or she may experience more emotional closeness with persons in the group than with his or her spouse while the group meets. Remind group members that Face-to-Face Support Groups exist to bring healing, not harm, to family life. Encourage members to be careful of the close relationships they may form in the group. Do not discourage friendships and emotional bonding. Perhaps the best guideline is to tell group members, "Male-female friendships formed in the group should not be nurtured outside the group in any way that minimizes or eliminates the involvement of both individuals' spouses."

If your sessions occur in the evening and tend to run late, another guideline to consider is that group members will go home immediately after the group session unless the whole group goes somewhere together. If it is appropriate for the group to go out for coffee after the session, plan this time in advance for the consideration of family members.

What if someone quits the group? Facing a painful past hurts. Some individuals waver to the last minute on their decision to join the group. The pain of the past seems overwhelming and frightening. The individual joins the group but soon is overwhelmed by what he discovers about himself. He may try to blame on others his fear and frustration. He may turn on you or on the whole group. He may claim that you are not spiritual. Utilize the whole group to respond calmly to this kind of criticism. Resist temptation to condemn. Be patient.

You will not always succeed in helping a person who responds to the group in this manner. Such a person may choose to quit the group. If so, call the person soon after he quits. Let him know that you are not offended and that he may call you in the future to talk about issues that may trouble him. You may want to ask, "How can I pray for you in the weeks ahead?" Offer to pray over the phone for the person. Ask God to comfort, to strengthen, and to demonstrate His love. Be reluctant to try talking the person into coming back. Try to leave an open door so that this individual may participate in another Face-To-Face Support Group.

If someone quits the group, use some time in the next session to let the group talk about it. Your purpose will not be character assassination but will be a chance to process the group's feelings and to learn about the experience.

What if family members don't understand? Families of group members are not always supportive. Besides having grown up in dysfunctional families, group members may be living in severely dysfunctional families now. Talking about issues threatens a dysfunctional-family system. It breaks the rule of silence. The family member's involvement in the group may threaten other family members.

Group members feel worse before they feel better, so family members may question whether the group really is helping. They even may fear that the group is making things worse.

When emotional distance exists in family relationships, fears may exist about this person's getting close to anyone else. The dysfunctional rule is "I don't want to get emotionally close to you, but I don't want anyone else to be emotionally close to you either."

Warn your group members that their families might not support their participation. Tell family members that group members tend to get worse before they get better. Explain to family members that the group is dealing with each person's family of origin and is not discussing the problems of current family members. Tell group members they can refer their family members and friends to *Family and Friends: Helping the Person You Care About in Recovery*, by Larry O. Pillow. This LIFE® Support Group Series course will help explain what a support group is and why people participate in it.

What if someone is not helped by the group? Some group members will gain more benefits than will others. Most persons who complete your group will indicate that they have been helped. Occasionally, someone may not show much improvement. How will you deal with this situation? First, realize that no one is perfect except God. Your group is not perfect. Also, not everyone will receive the same benefits from the group. Second, realize that some persons will need referral to a professional counselor because they need more help than your group can give. Some group members may ask if they can go through another Face-to-Face Support Group. The answer is yes. Some members want to go through the group again with the new understanding they gained from the first study.

For help in dealing with additional problems, read the *LIFE Support Leader's Handbook*. The *Handbook* can be downloaded at no charge from the Web site *http:// www.lifeway.com/download.asp.*

Training Potential Group Facilitators

Facilitators of Face-to-Face Support Groups participate with their group during the sessions. Before leading a group they will benefit by experiencing the course and by being involved in a variety of group experiences.

Conference Description

The following three-to-five hour teaching plan is to be used to help orient potential facilitators to *Making Peace with Your Past* in a state, or in a larger region.

This conference overviews the administrative material in this facilitator's guide and involves participants experientially in one group session.

Persons planning to lead *Making Peace with Your Past* in their churches should attend this conference. These persons may be pastors, other church-staff members, ministers of counseling or family life, church discipleship leaders, church family-enrichment committee members, deacons or elders, or other interested lay leaders.

Purpose and Outcomes

The purpose of this conference is to equip participants to lead *Making Peace with Your Past* in their local congregation. After completing the conference, qualified participants will be able to:

1. Describe *Making Peace with Your Past*;
2. Recognize the educational design of *Making Peace with Your Past*;
3. Describe the role and qualifications of the facilitator; and
4. Plan, promote, and facilitate *Making Peace with Your Past* in their church.

Before the Conference

❏ 1. Provide each participant a copy each of the facilitator's guide and member's book before the conference. Ask them to read pages 5-30 in the facilitator's guide and to work through unit 1 in the member's book before the conference.
❏ 2. Set up the meeting room. Place the chairs in circles with six to eight chairs in each circle.
❏ 3. Print each of the 10 foundational concepts for group process on a separate index card. Tape each one under a participant's chair.

❏ 4. Prepare a chart using the information highlighted in Step 10 below.
❏ 5. Provide name tags, markers, blank paper, and pencils for participants.

Conference Plan

1. **Getting Started** (10 minutes). Ask the participants to make a name tag, join a small group, begin getting acquainted, and compose a group definition of *recovery* and *dysfunctional* families.

2. **Telling Your Story** (20 minutes). Welcome the participants. Tell your story of making peace with your past. If this is not possible, tell Tim Sledge's story found in the member's book. This time is intended to model the role of a facilitator, your trust in the group, and your willingness to share your recovery journey. The more open you are, the better participants will be to lead groups in the future.

3. **Feeling Check** (10 minutes). Ask the participants to identify their feelings with one word, such as *sadness, fear, guilt, shame, joy, anger, pain, hope,* or *peace*. Affirm those willing to share.

4. **Goals of the Group** (20 minutes). Ask the participants to turn to page 10 of the facilitator's guide. Assign one of the "Goals for a Face-to-Face Support Group" to each person in each small group. Some persons may have more than one goal. After giving a minute for each person to prepare a summary of the goal, ask participants to share the goals in their small groups. Allow time for each goal to be described in the small group. Field and answer any questions the participants may have about the goals of a group.

5. **How the Group Works** (10 minutes). Ask the group to look in the member's book at the four ideas in "How a Support Group Works" (p. 26) and at the four ideas in "Keys to the Group Process" (pp. 26-27). Briefly discuss each idea. Discuss "Review of Group Assumptions and Procedures" in the member's book, p. 28.

6. **Break** (10 minutes).

7. **Experiencing session 1 (65 minutes)**. Ask the small groups to discuss responses to the four questions in the facilitator's guide (p. 32). Ask them to discuss

one question before moving to another question. Encourage the participants to share in any order they choose. Remind them that individuals are not required to speak, but all are encouraged to do so. Ask groups to keep track of the time and try to cover each question if possible.

8. **Debriefing session 1** (10 minutes). To debrief the experience ask the participants to reflect on the "Self-Evaluation Checklist" on the inside back cover of the facilitator's guide.

9. **Foundational concepts for group process** (15 minutes). Ask the participants to look under their chairs and find "Foundational Concepts for the Group Process." As each person reads a concept, comment on the point, summarizing the material in that topic in the facilitator's guide (pp. 12-18). Accept and respond to questions as time allows.

10. **Group-Session Overview** (15 minutes). Briefly describe each element in the session plan.
    1. Session Goal
    2. What to Expect
    3. Skills Development
    4. Before the Session
    5. During the Session
       • checking in
       • sharing-only format
       • discussion-question format
       • feeling check
       • closing the session
    6. After the Session

11. **Steps for Starting a Group** (30 minutes). Direct the participants' attention to "Steps for Starting a Face-to-Face Support Group," beginning on page 5-9 in the facilitator's guide. Divide the content of the steps evenly among the groups or individuals. Some groups or individuals will have to cover more than one step. Ask participants to develop a creative way to present the step to the rest of the large group. Call for presentations and clarify any points not made clearly.

12. **Goal Setting** (10 minutes). Give each participant paper and a pencil. Ask participants to write at least three things they want to do with this material/training. Call on volunteers to share their vision for a Face-to-Face Support Group ministry.

13. **Prayer Time** (10 minutes). Invite participants to pray in their small groups for each other and for the people facilitating this material across the country.

14. **Closure** (5 minutes). Summarize the conference and challenge participants to conduct *Making Peace with Your Past* as God leads them to do so. Close the session with prayer.

After the Conference

Write a follow-up letter to participants. Express appreciation for their attendance at the conference. Encourage them to conduct the course in their church and to let you know whether they need additional help or support.

Overview of Face-to-Face Group Sessions

The following group-session plans will help you guide meaningful sharing times for your Face-to-Face Support Group. Here is an overview of what you will find on the following pages:

Session Goal. The goal describes an anticipated outcome of the session. Keep in mind that members will progress at their own unique pace. Do not get discouraged if the goals are not achieved each week. The group members are your ministry. Be sensitive to their needs and allow the Lord to guide you in meeting those needs. What He wants to do in their lives may surpass any goal you may set for the session. Pray regularly that God will be your constant Guide throughout this process.

What to Expect. Based on my experience as a Face-to-Face facilitator, I have provided you with insights about what may happen during your sessions for each week. Based on the content the members are studying, new experiences will confront you week after week. These paragraphs are designed to alert you to potential experiences that may arise during the session.

Skill Development. I have made the assumption that you already have the basic skills required of a group facilitator. These suggestions each week are designed as continuing education for you. Take time to review the basic skills on the page number listed. Then observe my suggestions for practicing or fine-tuning your skill during the session.

Before the Session. If you will read through this list carefully and will complete each of the actions, you should be ready for the group session. Place a check mark beside each item as you complete it. Most of these actions are repeated from week to week so they will become routine by the end of the 12 weeks.

Notice that you prepare a "Feelings" poster for use the first week. Keep that poster and use it each week. You may want to get an artist to prepare an attractive poster and to have it laminated for use in this and in future Face-to-Face Support Groups.

Each week the sessions will encourage you to review the self-evaluation checklist on the inside back cover. This is placed for ready reference. Be sure to take time before each session to mentally walk through the list.

During the Session. A standard Face-to-Face group session includes: arrival activities, checking in, optional discussion questions, a feeling check, and a closing circle of prayer.

I have provided you with two formats for use in the sessions. One is a sharing-only format. To use this format you will begin with the checking-in process. A box on the inside back cover lists the questions you might use and the five areas that members may consider for sharing. If you need additional help, one or more "Checking In" questions are listed in a box under "During the Session."

A discussion-question format is a second option. To follow this format, begin with checking in to see if a member has a pressing problem or issue with which you need to deal. Then to prompt the group to begin sharing use the discussion questions in the box under "During the Session."

Make sure you move to the feeling check 15 to 30 minutes before the normal ending time. This should provide ample time to tie up any loose ends and to close with a circle of prayer.

Throughout the session, watch for times that the Lord may impress you to stop and to allow the group to pray for a member. God will work through the members of the group to comfort, challenge, or encourage a needy member. This is a practical way to keep your group Christ-centered.

After the Session. This check list is designed to help you evaluate the session and to begin preparing for the following session. Check each of the items as you complete it. I encourage you not to skip the process of keeping a journal. It will prove to be a valuable tool for skill building and will assist your memory about members' needs and about their progress as you pray for those in your group. I also encourage you to follow up each week by contacting your apprentice. He or she will help you evaluate the session more objectively. "Two heads always are better than one."

May the Lord work through you in a wonderful way to bring His healing to the painful memories of your group members. As a leader, keep in mind: "I can't. God can. I am going to let Him." Give Him the credit and the glory when He does!

Discovering Self-esteem

➤ Session Goal

Each person will become acquainted with other group members and will develop an awareness of common problems group members experience.

What to Expect

The first session of your group will set the tone for all future sessions. This session should communicate the message "We have come here to talk about something that is very hard to talk about, but we are going to start talking about it now." You can expect that some persons in your group will share experiences they never have shared with a group. You can anticipate that strong emotions will accompany this type of sharing.

You may feel fear and apprehension in the room before the sharing time begins. Remember, this is a giant step for most persons in the group. Dysfunctional families live under the no-talk rule. These persons have come to the group to break that rule, and they feel afraid. This session may last longer than subsequent sessions because each person needs to tell a part of his story.

Skill Development

Before the first session take time to reread the section "Basic Skills for Group Leadership" in this guide. Give special attention to the following skills and place a check beside each one as you complete your review.

❏ **1. Be personally involved without relinquishing leadership (p. 19).** Your attitude and involvement during the first session will set the tone for the way each group member shares in this session and in future sessions. During this session each group member will be asked to share his answers to the four groups of questions at the end of unit 1, day 5. You will begin by sharing your responses. Your honesty and emotional involvement will set the example for the other group members. As you share, you may become emotional. Don't worry about that. You are modeling what you want your group members to do. Of course, you do not want to act from an emotional response you

do not feel. Be yourself, but be willing to share something that hurts.

❏ **2. Communicate acceptance and concern (p. 19).** Group members will share painful truths during the session. Some of them will talk openly about things they seldom or never talk about. They will feel afraid and vulnerable. Your attitude and actions can create an atmosphere of acceptance and concern. When a group member is sharing and has to stop because he is crying, say: "I support you. It is OK to cry. This is a safe place to talk about this." Some group members will feel great shame about the things they are talking about. Some may feel ashamed even to be present in the group. Be open to ways to communicate an attitude of love and acceptance to each person.

❏ **3. Create a feeling of safety in the group (p. 20).** Remind the group that all that takes place in the group sessions is confidential. Affirm your commitment to maintaining confidentiality. If you have a counselor who is supervising you, mention that you sometimes will need to confer with that person on issues arising from the group sessions. Affirm your supervisor's commitment to confidentiality, as well.

Communicate confidence through the way you lead the group. You can be open about your own emotional pain while you still show that you are confident about your leadership.

When the session starts, make sure all doors to the room are closed. You may need to put some "Meeting in Progress" signs on doors to prevent interruptions.

Explain to the group members that they do not have to be Christians to participate in the group but that the group will include references to Christ's power to help with their emotional problems. Unchurched group members may fear that you somehow will pressure them to accept your beliefs. Your comments at this time can allay such fears. Unbelieving group members often are won to Christ when they over time experience the nonmanipulative love of a support group.

❏ **4. Keep the group operating on a feeling level (p. 23).** If all your Face-to-Face Support Group accomplishes is to have intellectual discussions on dysfunctional family issues, this will not help much. The first goal of the group is to help group members get in touch with their feelings. This session is a model for all the other sessions. The group needs to operate on a feeling level in this session. Usually, this happens naturally as people unload the pain of childhood traumas they long have held inside. Again, you are the key. You will set the tone by how you share your own story.

Before the Session

❏ Check the church calendar to be certain no one else is scheduled to use the room where your group will be meeting.

❏ If you are providing child care, make sure the child-care workers are prepared to stay as late as necessary. The first session often runs longer than do other sessions.

❏ Place directional signs at all outside church entrances leading to your meeting room.

❏ Make sure the temperature for air conditioning or heating is set properly.

❏ Be sure the room is clean, with the exact number of chairs needed arranged in a circle.

❏ Place several boxes of tissue around the circle.

❏ Have a legal pad and a pen for taking notes.

❏ Prepare a reusable name tag for each group member. For custom name tags photocopy the name tags on page 34 on colored card stock, and cut them apart. Provide plastic holders for these tags or provide masking tape each week.

❏ Write the following on poster board so that everyone will be able to see, or have the full-page illustration on page 62 enlarged to poster size. Save this poster for use in each session.

Feelings

• **Anger**	• **Fear**
• **Guilt**	• **Joy**
• **Loneliness**	• **Sadness**
•**Shame**	• **Other**

❏ Photocopy the "Face-to-Face Support Group Affirmations" (p. 64) on card stock and provide one affirmation card for each group member. Cut apart and fold the cards. Consider covering the cards with clear plastic adhesive shelf covering for durability.

During the Session

1. **Arrival.** Greet the group members as they arrive for the session. Give each member a card listing the Face-to-Face affirmations.
2. **Name tags.** Give each person a name tag.
3. **Start.** Start the session at the scheduled time.
4. **Review the covenant.** Review the covenant that each member signed. Emphasize that confidentiality is necessary.
5. **Sharing/discussion questions.** During this first session the format will be the same, whether you are using the sharing-only format or the discussion-question format. Each person will be asked to share his or her answers to the four groups of questions on pages 28-29 in the member book. The questions are:

Discussion Questions for Week 1

• Did you come from a dysfunctional family? Why do you think the family was dysfunctional?

• Why are you participating in this group? What issue in your life brought you here?

• Describe one incident that would help us understand what it felt like to grow up in your family. It may have been a hurt, a humiliation, or a horror.[1]

• What goals do you want to accomplish in this group?

Before you begin sharing, explain to group members that you will be taking notes as they speak. Tell them that this is a privilege reserved for the group facilitator. Ask them to have nothing, including their books, in their hands or laps during the session.

You will share your answers to the questions first. Answer the fourth question in terms of something you are working on personally, not in terms of your role as a facilitator. After you have shared, call on someone else to share. Don't go around the circle. Ask someone to volunteer or choose a person who seems ready to share.

As the group members share, take notes on a legal pad. You will not take notes during any other session. You need to make notes during this session because what the group members share in this session will become the foundation for the rest of the work they do. Your notes will help you remember the key details of each person's story. Do not stop anyone who is sharing because you are behind on your notes, but write down what you can. Work hard to look at the person who is talking, even though you are taking notes. Try to be a good listener while you are taking notes.

Here's an example of how the first session might start.

I begin by telling group members my name. They probably already know my name since I am the facilitator, but I am modeling what I want them to do.

I tell the group that I grew up in a dysfunctional family. My family was dysfunctional because it focused its attention on an addictive family member, my father, who was an alcoholic. He stopped drinking sometime during my teenage years and made many positive changes in his life, but our family continued to operate under many dysfunctional patterns. Our family was rather closed to the outside world. We did not have a feasible plan for solving emotional or relational problems. I tell the group that I am here not just because I have the responsibility of leading the group. I am here because my father was an alcoholic, and I have discovered that his alcoholism affected my life in negative ways. I explain that the first time I participated in such a group, I needed help in dealing with anxiety and panic attacks.

I describe an incident from my childhood:

I was about 11. My father had not come home. We did not know where he was. My sister, 7 years old, and I had climbed into bed with my mom. We all felt scared. We loved my dad and felt frightened for him. Finally, I fell asleep. I was awakened in the middle of the night. I don't remember if I was awakened by the sound on the other side of the room or by what my mother was saying. The sound was that of my father's urinating on the bedroom floor. He was drunk and did not know where he was. My mother was saying something to him, and her voice conveyed anger and pain. (I show pain as I tell the incident. It still hurts, and it hurts to tell about it.)

Finally, I tell the group something I want to work on in this group. For example, I might share that I am going to work on letting myself feel happy without letting other people determine my happiness or the lack of it.

I stop. I ask for a volunteer to share his or her answers in the same four areas. Or if I see that someone is about to burst with emotion, I may ask that person, "Are you ready to share?" A person who is ready to release a torrent of emotion just by telling some simple facts about the pain of her childhood will help other group members who are not yet in touch with their feelings.

Someone else begins to share, then another and another. The members of the group share at different levels. Each group is different. In some groups a person may relate a heart-wrenching incident, and many members of the group break down. They have been hurting all their lives. They have kept secrets. They can hold the pain inside no longer. In other groups the first session is not characterized by such dramatic emotions. Even when the first session is somewhat calm, you still will feel a sense of emotional intensity in what is happening.

Estimate how much time you have for each person to share. Don't rush anyone, but if a group member takes too much time, step in to encourage and redirect her toward a conclusion.

6. Feeling check. After every member has shared, commend the group members for their sharing. If you have time, conduct a feeling check. Point to the different emotions named on the poster "Feelings" and ask group members which feeling they are experiencing now.

Tell the group members that they may experience fear about coming back to the next session. Remind them that because they have broken the rule of silence, they may feel frightened. Encourage them to stay with the process, which can lead to healing.

Distribute copies of the group roster with the phone numbers of the group members who have given permission for other group members to call them. The roster also should contain your phone number. Encourage group members to call one another for support. Let them know that they can call you if they have questions during the week. Remind the group members to complete the five daily assignments in unit 2 before the next session.

7. Circle of prayer. Ask group members to stand and join hands. Invite each member to say a sentence prayer either thanking God for something that happened in the group or asking for God's help with an issue related to the focus of the group. Each person should pray about himself, not about someone else in the group or outside the group.

After the Session

❏ Collect the name tags and save the poster "Feelings" for use in the remaining sessions.
❏ Mark attendance on the group roster.

> Because so much group bonding takes place during the first session, it would be better for anyone who missed the first session to wait for the course to be offered again.

❏ Look over the notes you took during the session. Pray for each member. Keep the notes for later prayer and review.
❏ If someone signed up for the group but did not attend the first session, contact him.
❏ Consider keeping a journal during the time you are leading the group. Start now by describing your feelings about leading the group. What emotions did you feel as you led the first session? What questions do you have that presently are unanswered?

❏ Evaluate your facilitation. You may want to write responses to the following questions as a part of your skill building. If you keep a journal, record your answers there.
  • Was I personally and emotionally involved without relinquishing leadership? How?
  • What did I do to communicate acceptance and concern?
  • What did I do to create a feeling of safety in the group?
  • Did I keep the group operating on a feeling level? What indicates that the group operated on a feeling level?

❏ Contact your apprentice or assistant group facilitator, if you have one, and discuss his or her responses to the session.
❏ Begin preparation for the next session.
❏ Call group members this week to affirm their participation. If you detect a member is hesitant to continue, encourage him to continue in the process as he moves toward healing.

[1]David A. Seamands, *Healing of Memories* (Wheaton: Victor Books, 1985), 79-93.

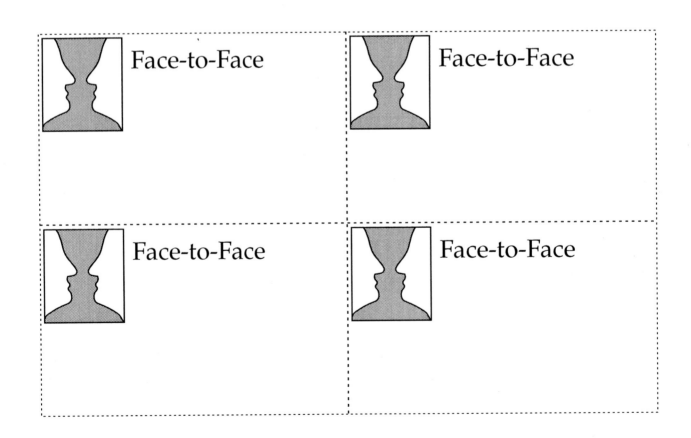

Face-to-Face

Face-to-Face

Face-to-Face

Face-to-Face

Recognizing Compulsive Behavior

> ➤ **Session Goal**
>
> Group members will be able to help one another by giving feedback during the group session.

What to Expect

Some group members will be surprised and frightened as they think about how much they shared during the first session. Some may consider quitting the group because it may seem too dangerous. Persons who have lived all their lives in denial do not move to openness easily. Persons who have become proficient at keeping secrets are frightened by the idea of talking openly about family pain. You can expect some group members to feel that they said too much last week. They may be uncertain about how far they want to go with the group process.

Even group members who have questions about having said too much probably will share in this positive feeling that characterizes the group: "At last I have found a place to talk about my pain. I feel better because I feel hope. I am starting to think that this may be a safe place."

Some group members may have been able to admit for the first time that they came from dysfunctional families. A group member who has just admitted this to herself will feel grief. This grief signifies that she has begun to let go of an idealized view of her family, and it will require some adjustment.

Skill Development

Work on three skills this week.

❏ **1. Teach group members how to help one another (p. 25).** Remind the group members of the following guidelines.

- When a group member is struggling, say, "I support you." Group members may say this at any time. It is not necessary for the facilitator to give a cue in order for group members to give each other feedback.

- After a group member has shared, be willing to give feedback. Listen to your feelings as well as your thoughts. What were you feeling when the group member was sharing? Your feelings may help the group member identify what he was feeling. If the facilitator does not ask you to give feedback, it is OK to ask the individual, "May I give some feedback?" With the permission of the facilitator and the person to whom you are offering the feedback, you may proceed.

- Think about how you phrase your statements. "I feel that you are experiencing a lot of fear about being in the group today" is better than "You're obviously afraid of this group."

- If the person sitting next to you is struggling, express concern. For example, you might gently place your hand on this person's shoulder.

- Remind the group that you as the facilitator will guide the session. Group members need to take their cues from what you do and say. At the same time, they can take the initiative to offer help to one another.

❏ **2. Facilitate feedback (p. 21).**

❏ **3. Help group members identify what they are feeling (p. 22).**

Before the Session

❏ If you have not done so, call group members to let them know that you are looking forward to seeing them at the second session.

❏ Review the notes you took on each group member's responses during the first session and pray for each member.

❏ Check the room environment. Be sure the room is clean, with the exact number of chairs you need arranged in a circle. Make sure the air conditioning or heating is set properly. Have several boxes of tissue ready. Make this standard check of the room environment each week.

❏ Display the poster "Feelings," which you prepared for Session 1.

❏ If you are using the discussion-question format, you may want to write the discussion questions on a chalkboard or on poster board.

❑ Review the self-evaluation checklist on the inside back cover.

During the Session

1. Arrival. Greet the group members as they arrive; distribute name tags; and start on time.

2. Checking in. Begin by letting the group members check in. Explain that *checking in* means giving a brief report, which could focus on any one of several areas:

• What has happened to me emotionally in response to the previous group session?
• What am I feeling at the present time–anger? fear? guilt? joy? loneliness? sadness? shame?
• How do I feel about the group process?
• Does any pressing emotional or spiritual pain need to be dealt with immediately?
• What is my initial reaction to the material we studied this week?

Start the check-in time by asking, "Does anyone have anything pressing that you need to share today?" or "What happened in your life this past week as a result of our previous session?"

Let the first issue raised lead into issues that other group members mention. What one person shares will raise certain issues in the lives of other group members. As they describe their issues, you can lead the group to respond to them. You can build the whole session around responses to the needs group members identify. Having completed the week's assignments, they will reflect what they have learned in the issues they raise.

This format requires courage and faith for you as the leader. You could call it "flying by the seat of your pants." Or you could call it leaning on the Spirit of God.

An important principle in keeping the group moving is to ask group members, "What are you feeling?" after another group member has shared. Challenge the group members to register a feeling response, using one of the words listed on the poster "Feelings." If the group member you ask is not able to identify a feeling, keep talking. Ask him again. Or ask him why he feels nothing. Do not assume a hostile attitude. You should press just hard enough to move past the wall of denial and emotional numbness. If a group member is still not able to identify a feeling, ask another group member what feelings he detects from the group member who is unable to identify his feelings.

The study material for the week or something that happened during or since the previous group session may raise intense issues. A group member may need to talk about such an issue as soon as the group begins. Start the session by responding to any pressing issue that group members raise during the initial period of checking in. Consider using these questions during the check-in period.

Checking In for Week 2

• Did any of you consider not returning to the group? Why?
• What feelings have you had since the first session? Refer to the list on the poster "Feelings."
• Do you have questions about whether you grew up in a dysfunctional family? If so, what are they?

In the sharing-only format let the issues group members raise lead to further sharing. Keep the group on a feeling level.

3. Discussion-question format. If you are using discussion questions, limit the check-in time to allow discussion of the questions below. These are more questions than you will be able to cover in one session.

Discussion Questions for Week 2

• Are you engaging in compulsive behavior? In what way?
• Can you recognize ways your compulsive behavior keeps you from feeling certain emotions? If so, describe how.
• Did your family of origin feel out of control when you were a child? If so, describe what made it feel out of control.
• Do you have a need to be in control? If so, what do you try to control?
• Do you have compulsive or addictive behavior in your life that hurts your relationship with God or with other persons? Explain.
• Do you have compulsive behavior in your life that makes you tired? Explain.

As group members respond to the questions, remember to keep the group operating on a feeling level. Use questions like "How does that make you feel?" Ask group members to respond by choosing one of the emotions from the list on the poster "Feelings."

4. Feeling check. Between 15 and 30 minutes before the session is scheduled to adjourn, conduct a feeling check. Point to the different emotions listed on the poster and ask group members which feelings they are experiencing now. Remind the group members to complete the five daily assignments in unit 3 before the next session.

5. Circle of prayer. Ask group members to stand and join hands. Invite each group member to say a sentence prayer either thanking God for something that happened in the group or asking for God's help with an issue related to the focus of the group. Each person should pray about himself, not about someone else in the group or outside the group.

After the Session

❏ Collect the name tags.
❏ Mark attendance on the group roster.
❏ Record in your journal your thoughts and feelings about the session.
❏ Evaluate your skill-building work by answering the following questions. Record appropriate responses in your journal.
  • What did I do to teach group members to help one another in the group process?
  • What indicates that group members were learning to help one another in the group process?
  • What did I do to facilitate feedback in the group?
  • Did I help group members learn to give feedback to one another?
❏ Contact your apprentice or assistant group facilitator to evaluate the session.

"Cast all your Anxiety on him because he cares for you"

Accept God's Love for me   God is in (Control)   I Pet 5:7

Release from Shame

> ## ➤ Session Goal
>
> Group members will identify and understand ways internalized shame may be affecting their thoughts and behavior.

What to Expect

Shame may be the most pervasive emotion members of your group confront. You can anticipate that the topic for this meeting will be close to the core of the members' emotional struggles.

Members of your group have started the journey away from denial toward facing the truth about their families. They may feel some sadness and depression. Assure them that people normally feel worse before they feel better. Explain that anyone who has been denying buried emotional pain will feel worse when she first begins to uncover it. She can expect to feel better as she continues to face these feelings because feelings lose their power when people remove them from the closet of denial.

Another reason for sadness at this point is grief. When a group member who has spent his life denying the existence or the extent of family problems begins to admit that his family was filled with emotional pain and turmoil, a form of grief will follow. The individual has lost the mythical family his denial has created. Such a loss produces grief.

Skills Development

Review the following three skills in preparation for this session.

❏ **1. Be willing to confront in love (p. 19).** Remember that you cannot effectively lead this group if you are unwilling to confront. If you habitually avoid conflict, you will not be effective as the facilitator of the group.

Watch for signs of denial. For example, a group member says that he does not have a problem with shame. But in each of the previous sessions this group member has apologized, "I'm sorry for crying" and "I'm sorry I

took so much time to share my story." You sense that this individual feels sorry for existing. You wait for the right opportunity, and you say, "Jim, you are telling us that you do not have a problem with shame, but you are communicating a lot of shame when you apologize for things that require no apology."

At this point the group member may respond by continuing in denial. If he does, ask him, "Would you be willing for other group members to give you feedback?" With his permission ask other group members to comment on whether they spot shame in his life. If several agree with you, ask him to respond again.

Maybe he will start to listen. When he does, you can begin to explore the depth and the sources of his shame effectively.

❏ **2. Help group members connect the past with the present (p. 22).**

❏ **3. Keep the group operating on a feeling level (p. 23).** Remember that powerful expressions of emotion may occur in your group. When someone begins to cry, give him time to cry. Do not change the subject. Do not turn the discussion to another group member. Do not say, "It's OK; don't cry." Let the person cry for a while. Use statements like "It's OK to cry. It's OK to feel your emotions. This is a safe place to cry." Observe how other group members react to this person's crying. Some obviously will feel their own emotions.

A key element in keeping the group on a feeling level is your willingness to stay in touch with your own feelings. If you refuse to allow yourself to feel your emotions, the group will follow your lead. Feel free to say at various points in the meeting, "I am feeling some sadness" or "I am feeling some fear right now."

Before the Session

❏ Review the notes you took on each group member's responses during the first session and pray for each member.
❏ Check the room environment (see p. 35).
❏ Display the poster "Feelings."

- ❏ If you are using the discussion-question format, you may want to write the discussion questions on a chalkboard or on poster board.
- ❏ Review the self-evaluation checklist on the inside back cover.

During the Session

1. Arrival. Greet the group members as they arrive; distribute name tags; and start on time.

2. Checking in. Begin by letting the group members check in. Explain again what *checking in* means (see p. 24).

Start the check-in time by asking, "Does anyone have anything pressing that he or she needs to share today?" or "What happened in your life this past week as a result of our previous session?" Consider using these questions during the check-in period.

Checking In for Week 3

- Do you have a shame-based identity?
- How is shame affecting your thoughts and your behavior?

In the sharing-only format let the first issue raised lead into issues that other group members mention. What one person shares will raise certain issues in the lives of other group members. As they describe their issues, you can lead the group to respond to them. You can build the whole session around responses to the needs group members identify. Having completed the week's assignments, group members will reflect what they have learned in the issues they raise.

A reminder: An important principle in keeping the group moving is to ask group members, "What are you feeling?" after another group member has shared. Challenge the group members to register a feeling response, using one of the words you listed on the chalkboard earlier. If the group member you ask is not able to identify a feeling, keep talking. Ask him again. Or ask him why he feels nothing. Do not assume a hostile attitude. Be forceful. You should press just hard enough to move past the wall of denial and emotional numbness. If a group member still is not able to identify a feeling, ask another group member what feelings he detects from the group member who is unable to identify his feelings.

3. Discussion-question format. If you are using discussion questions, limit the check-in time to allow discussion of the questions below. These are more questions than you will be able to cover in one session.

Discussion Questions for Week 3

- Did your family transmit shame to you? If so, list some ways this was done.
- How has shame affected your choices of persons for close relationships?
- What methods have you used to deny shame?
- Do you transmit shame to persons around you?

As group members respond to the questions, remember to keep the group operating on a feeling level. Use questions like "How does that make you feel?" Ask group members to respond by choosing one of the emotions from the list on the poster "Feelings."

4. Feeling check. Between 15 and 30 minutes before the session is scheduled to adjourn, conduct a feeling check. Point to the different emotions the poster lists and ask group members which feelings they are experiencing now. Remind the group members to complete unit 4's five daily assignments before the next session.

5. Circle of prayer. Ask group members to stand and join hands. Invite each group member to say a sentence prayer for the person on his right, asking God to help this person win a victory over shame.

After the Session

- ❏ Collect the name tags.
- ❏ Mark attendance on the group roster.
- ❏ Record in your journal your thoughts and feelings about the session.
- ❏ Evaluate your skill-building work by answering the following questions. Record appropriate responses in your journal.
  - In this week's session did you confront a group member? If so, how did you communicate love and acceptance as you confronted?
  - Describe an incident in this session in which you helped a group member connect shame from the past with a present problem. How did you accomplish this?
  - What did you do during this session to keep the group operating on a feeling level?
- ❏ Contact your apprentice or assistant group facilitator to evaluate the session.

Overcoming the Fear of Joy

➤ Session Goal

Group members will identify and understand ways a fear of success and happiness may be keeping them from reaching their full potential.

What to Expect

Group members now should be feeling more comfortable in the group. Most of them should look forward to the sessions. Having learned to anticipate receiving help, they are becoming interested in providing support for the other group members. The group is starting to feel like a warm and safe place. Some group members still may struggle with feelings that they are a part of the group. Many of the group members have spent lifetimes perceiving themselves as being on the outside of close relationships. Keep reminding each group member that he or she is as much a part of the group as is any group member. Be sensitive to persons who seem to have special difficulty.

Some people may be considering sharing a major secret that they never have discussed with anyone. These people feel a mixture of fear and hope. They want to break the silence, but the possibility is extremely frightening. Keep working to create a feeling of safety in the group. Give reticent group members time to make up their own minds about sharing long-kept secrets.

Group members still may have a sense of feeling worse instead of better. This hurt is a normal part of the process. Help group members understand the increased level of emotional pain they may be feeling.

Last week some group members discovered that they have shame-based identities. The implications of this concept still are unfolding for them. They may have more questions about shame this week. Be willing to adjust the session agenda if necessary.

This week's session deals with the fear of happiness and success. Persons who have shame-based identities do not feel that they deserve happiness or success. Help group members see the connection between shame and a fear of joy.

Skill Development

Review the skill-building subjects on the pages listed below.

❏ **1. Integrate biblical and psychological truth (p. 23).** The biblical basis for this unit is "You did not receive a spirit that makes you a slave again to fear" (Romans 8:15, NIV).[1] Group members may have a sound, rational understanding of a loving God who encourages joy while they have a poor heartfelt impression of who God is. A god who induces shame and prohibits joy is not the living God! This week you will want to help group members accept the grace of God at an experiential level. Help them feel God's love and acceptance through the love and acceptance the group displays. Take the lead by modeling caring acceptance of each group member.

❏ **2. Utilize good listening skills (p. 25).** Work on these skills:

- When one group member speaks, visually scan the other group members occasionally. What are they saying nonverbally?
- Remember occasionally to restate and summarize what a group member has just said to the group. Then ask, "Is that what you said?" Let the group member respond.
- Remember to face the person who is speaking and to lean toward the speaker.
- When appropriate, nod your head to show that you are hearing what is being said. Use an occasional verbal phrase to indicate that you are listening.
- When necessary, stop the speaker and ask for clarification of what was just said.
- Make sure that someone in the group responds when a person says something that needs a response.

❏ **3. Know how to end a session (p. 24).** Occasionally, a group member may surprise you by saying something like "I'm not going to be able to stay much longer. I'm not feeling well." These words may carry a nonverbal message, "I am not willing to stay much longer, and I think you should end the session." If you are getting this message from several persons in the group, you may need to end the session. If the statement comes from one person, that person may need to control. The person may be afraid to face issues you are addressing. Encourage such a person to stay until the session is over. You may want to ask, "Is something about this session making you uncomfortable?" Do not let a controlling person manipulate the group by using such comments to determine when the session will end. You may need to say, "You may leave early while we stay to finish the session." If a group member tries to force an early end to more than one session, you will need to confront that individual. Do not permit a group member repeatedly to leave the session early.

Learn to be flexible about when to end the session, but do not consistently end it an hour later than the target time for adjourning. It is not unusual for a group session to last between two and three hours.

Before the Session

❏ Review the notes you took on each group member's responses during the first session and pray for each member.
❏ Check the room environment (see p. 35).
❏ Display the poster "Feelings."
❏ If you are using the discussion-question format, you may want to write the discussion questions on a chalkboard or on poster board.
❏ Review the self-evaluation checklist on the inside back cover.

During the Session

1. Arrival. Greet the group members as they arrive; distribute name tags; and start on time.

2. Checking in. Begin by letting the group members check in. Explain again what *checking in* means (see p. 24). Remind members of the areas they may consider (listed on the inside back cover).

Start the check-in time by asking, "Does anyone have anything pressing that he or she needs to share today?" or "What happened in your life this past week as a result of our previous session?" Consider using these questions during the check-in period.

Checking In for Week 4

• Did your family teach you to fear joy?
• If so, what were some ways your family taught you to fear joy?

In the sharing-only format let the first issue raised lead into other issues that group members mention. What one person shares will raise certain issues in the lives of other group members. As they describe their issues, you can lead the group to respond to them. Let the group propel itself in this manner.

It is not necessary for you to know exactly where the group will end when the session concludes. The group process will produce an agenda that unfolds step-by-step through the session.

3. Discussion-question format. If you are using discussion questions, limit the check-in time to allow discussion of the questions below. These are more questions than you will be able to cover in one session.

Discussion Questions for Week 4

• Have you ever sabotaged your own success? How?
• Was your ability to feel happy enmeshed with another family member's feelings? Who? How?
• How did your family of origin treat the future?

Keep the group operating on a feeling level.

4. Affirmations. Bring the group to a point of closure on the issues raised during the meeting. Ask group members if they are praying for one another daily but not in a way that brings shame. Encourage the group to be faithful in praying for one another every day.

Ask group members if they are saying aloud the affirmations each day. If some comment that they feel silly or even selfish saying them aloud, remind them of the importance of doing so. One of the first times I tried to say recovery affirmations aloud, I began to cry. Saying them aloud made me aware of how much I was hurting.

Affirmations are a significant way to replace old, negative thought patterns with new thoughts that are positive and full of faith.

Ask group members to turn to page 79 to the section "Giving Yourself Permission to Succeed" in their books. Lead them in saying aloud the 10 affirmations together.

5. Circle of prayer. Ask group members to stand and join hands. Invite each member to say a sentence prayer, thanking God for something that happened in this session and asking God for the freedom to be happy.

After the Session

❏ Collect the name tags.
❏ Mark attendance on the group roster.
❏ Record in your journal your thoughts and feelings about the session.
❏ Evaluate the way you closed the session.
  • Were you sensitive to the needs of the group in deciding when to close the session?
  • Did you bring each issue raised to a point of closure?
  • Were you sensitive to any unmet needs as you moved toward closing the session?
  • Did you encourage group members to introduce unfinished topics at the next session?
  • Did you stop the session after the circle of prayer?
  • Did you permit one group member to influence the time when the session ended?
❏ Contact your apprentice or assistant group facilitator to evaluate the session.
❏ Evaluate your skill-building work by answering the following questions. Record appropriate responses in your journal.
  • What did you do in this session to help group members develop a better understanding of God's grace and joy?
  • Place a check beside each of the listening skills below that you practiced during this session.
  • Were you sensitive to any unmet needs as you moved toward closing the session?
  • Did you encourage group members to introduce unfinished topics at the next session?
  • Did you stop the session after the circle of prayer?
  • Did you permit one group member to influence the time when the session ended?

Listening Skills

❏ When one group member is speaking, visually scan the other group members occasionally. What are they saying nonverbally?
❏ Remember occasionally to restate and summarize what a group member has just said to the group. Then ask, "Is that what you said?" Let the group member respond.
❏ Remember to face the person who is speaking and to lean toward the speaker.
❏ When appropriate, nod your head to show that you are hearing what someone is saying. Use an occasional verbal phrase to indicate that you are listening to what someone is saying..
❏ When necessary, stop the speaker and ask for clarification of what was just said.
❏ Make sure that someone in the group gives a response when a person says something that needs a response.

Help for People Who Grew Up Too Soon

> ## ➤ Session Goal
>
> Group members will identify and understand aspects of childhood that may have been lost in a dysfunctional family.

What to Expect

In this session you will work to help group members identify the emotional losses they experienced while growing up in dysfunctional families. As group members begin to identify the losses of childhood, they can begin to grieve for these losses. Working through the grief process sets the stage for moving ahead with life, for living in the present tense.

Group members need to understand that although they cannot relive their childhoods, they can reclaim child-like qualities that are crucial to emotionally healthy adult living. Another important aspect of this session is the focus on surrender to God. Some members of your group may come to realize that they have never surrendered their lives to God. Encourage them to make the spiritual commitment they need to make. Other group members may feel secure in knowing that they have made commitments to Christ while they feel that something is missing in their daily Christian walks. In either case you have an exciting opportunity to provide meaningful spiritual direction.

This week's topic could result in a group member's sharing an abuse experience that he did not share during the first session. Be ready for the possibility that some group members have not yet shared their most painful traumatic events.

Skill Development

Review the following skills in preparation for this session.

❏ **1. Help group members identify their feelings (p. 22).** Group members who acknowledge the losses of childhood will experience grief. Help group members call grief by its name. Help them to understand the components of grief: sadness, loss, and anger.

Assist group members in making statements like "I lost my childhood, and it feels sad."

When a group member describes a part of childhood that was lost, you can help by asking, "How does it feel to have lost that part of your childhood?" Point to the seven feelings listed on the poster "Feelings." Ask the group member if he has any of these feelings.

When a group member identifies basic childhood needs that were unmet, ask, "How did it feel when those needs were not met?" Point to the seven feelings listed on the poster "Feelings." Ask the group member if he had any of those feelings.

Help group members identify feelings that no one validated during his or her childhood. Help each group member connect the past with the present. For example, if a group member says that she was not allowed to be angry as a child, ask, "What do you do with your anger now?" Probe to discover this person's present pattern for dealing with anger.

❏ **2. Validate feelings (p. 26).**

❏ **3. Keep one person from dominating the group (p. 25).** By this point in the study you may have observed that one of your group members tends to dominate the group. Following is a list of ways a person may dominate a group.

- Claiming a major portion of each group session to talk about his issues
- Attempting to move the group toward an early dismissal if he or she is uncomfortable with what is happening
- Repeatedly waiting until the last 10 minutes of a session to drop an emotional bombshell
- Attempting to block other group members' expressions of emotions
- Making efforts to shame you as the group facilitator through repeated, hostile challenges to your leadership
- Criticizing the motives or feelings of other group members
- Repeatedly trying to rescue other group members who are in the midst of receiving needed confrontation.

The key in determining whether a group member is attempting to dominate the group is repeated behavior. A person may or may not be conscious of attempting to dominate the group. That is not the point. If you permit a group member to dominate group sessions, the group's effectiveness will be destroyed.

The first step in dealing with such a member is to challenge the behavior as it happens. Don't be hostile. Be confrontive. Here are some statements you might use:

- "Mary, we have spent a major part of the past three sessions dealing with the issue you just described. We need to focus on some other group members today."
- "Joe, our group agreed earlier on how long we will meet. We are following the plans we made. We need to continue with the session."
- "Chuck, this is the third time you have waited until the end of the session to introduce something that we need a lot of time to respond to. Why do you wait so long to bring up something so important?"
- "Kathleen, Mary needs to cry right now. When you tell her not to cry, you are making it hard for her to get better."

Another helpful method is to get feedback from other group members. Ask group members to comment on the behavior. For example, you might ask a question like, "James, how do you feel about Joe's request to end the session early today?" When you ask a question like this, ask someone who will be strong enough to give a healthy response.

If the problem persists, you may need to talk to the person one-to-one. You may need to encourage the individual to drop out of the group in order to engage in one-to-one counseling sessions. Hopefully, things will not go this far, but you should be willing to take the necessary steps to keep any group member from dominating the group in an unhealthy way.

Before the Session

❑ Review the notes you took on each group member's responses during the first session and pray for each member.
❑ Check the room environment (see p. 35).
❑ Display the poster "Feelings."
❑ If you are using the discussion-question format, you may want to write the discussion questions on a chalkboard or on poster board.
❑ Review the self-evaluation checklist on the inside back cover.

During the Session

1. Arrival. Greet the group members as they arrive; distribute name tags; and start on time.

2. Checking in. Begin by letting the group members check in. Remind members of the areas listed on the inside back cover.

Start the check-in time by asking, "Does anyone have anything pressing that he or she needs to share today?" or "What happened in your life this past week as a result of our previous session?" Consider using these questions during the check-in period.

Checking In for Week 5

- Did you lose part of your childhood? If so, what did you lose?
- Do you see yourself as an adult child? Why?

In the sharing-only format let the first issue raised lead into other issues that group members mention. What one person shares will raise certain issues in the lives of other group members. As they describe their issues, you can lead the group to respond to them. Let the group propel itself in this manner. It is not necessary for you to know exactly where the group will end when the session concludes. The group process will produce an agenda that unfolds step-by-step through the session.

Remember to stop for feeling checks throughout the session. Ask group members, "What are you feeling right now?" Follow the side roads that emerge from their responses.

3. Discussion-question format. If you are using discussion questions, limit the check-in time to allow discussion of the questions on the following page. These are more questions than you will be able to cover in one session.

As group members respond to these questions, remember to keep the group operating on a feeling level. Use questions like "How does that make you feel?"

Ask group members to respond by choosing one of the emotions from the list on the poster "Feelings."

4. Feeling check. Between 15 and 30 minutes before the session is scheduled to adjourn, conduct a feeling check. Point to the different emotions listed on the poster and ask group members which feelings they are experiencing now. Remind the group members to complete the five daily assignments in unit 6 before the next session.

Read the covenant that all group members signed at the beginning of the study. Remind group members of the commitments they made.

5. Circle of prayer. Ask each group member to thank God for something that happened during today's session.

After the Session

- ❏ Collect the name tags.
- ❏ Mark attendance on the group roster.
- ❏ Record in your journal your thoughts and feelings about the session.
- ❏ Evaluate your skill-building work by answering the following questions. Record appropriate responses in your journal.
  - What childhood losses did you help group members identify?
  - What feelings were associated with the childhood losses the group members identified?
  - Have you had a problem with one person's attempt to dominate the group? If so, how did you identify this problem?
  - What steps did you take during today's session to deal with the problem?
  - List three situations in today's session in which you validated a group member's feelings.
- ❏ Contact your apprentice or assistant group facilitator to evaluate the session.

Perfectionism and Procrastination

> ### ➤ Session Goal
>
> Group members will identify signs of perfectionist behavior in their lives.

What to Expect

By this time group members should be initiating more input and giving more feedback to one another. Allow group members to have an increasing level of input into the direction of each session.

Perfectionism is a powerful compulsion for many people. Often it is such a deep part of an individual's identity that its presence is strongly denied. Watch for denial and be prepared to confront it. Remember that perfectionism can be intertwined with an unhealthy religious legalism. Be ready for a powerful session.

Skills Development

Review the following skills in preparation for this session.

❏ **1. Facilitate feedback (p. 21).** This week give special attention to helping group members give feedback to one another. Some examples of statements you could make to facilitate feedback are:

- "What feelings seem to be present in our group right now?"
- "Sue, what did you feel when Lois said that her father had beaten her?"
- "I would like for about three of you to give Andy feedback on what he has said."

Watch the faces of group members as they listen to a member share. If you see strong emotion in a group member's facial expression or body language, ask that person for feedback.

❏ **2. Keep the group operating on a feeling level (p. 23).**

❏ **3. Stay ready for anything (p. 25).** If you are a person who needs to have everything planned, you will have to work on being spontaneous during the group sessions. Lean on God. Trust Him to help you.

❏ **4. Teach group members to help one another (p. 25).** The healing process for the group does not rest squarely on your shoulders. It rests in the hands of God. It also is found in the help that group members give to one another. Don't short-circuit the healing of the group process by trying to do it all yourself.

Remind group members to use the phrase "I support you" when another group member struggles. Encourage group members to offer a hug or another form of encouragement when appropriate.

Sometimes a group member may make a statement to another group member like "It is wrong for you to feel so angry." This is called invalidating a feeling. Group members should try to get in touch with feelings. It is dangerous to deny feelings and to proceed immediately to moral judgments. We must acknowledge our feelings and then take appropriate action to redirect our behavior. When one group member invalidates the feelings of another, focus on the group member who made the invalidating statement. Utilize the group process to help this group member discover his own issues, which are reflected in his attempt to suppress another member's feelings. Often the group member who invalidates someone else's feeling is having a fierce inner struggle with that feeling himself or with feelings in general.

Help group members understand why you respond to various group situations as you do. Begin asking yourself and God whether any of the members could lead groups in the future.

Before the Session

❏ Review the notes you took on each group member's responses during the first session and pray for each member.
❏ Check the room environment (see p. 35).
❏ Display the poster "Feelings."
❏ If you are using the discussion-question format, you may want to write the discussion questions on a chalkboard or on poster board.

During the Session

1. Arrival. Greet the group members as they arrive; distribute name tags; and start on time.

2. Checking in. Begin by letting the group members check in (see p. 24). Remind members of the areas for checking in (inside back cover).

Start the check-in time by asking, "Does anyone have anything pressing that he or she needs to share today?" or "What happened in your life this past week as a result of our previous session?" Consider using these questions during the check-in period.

Checking in for Week 6

- Are you a perfectionist? Do you have pockets of perfectionistic behavior?
- Have you tried to do things that only God can do?

In the sharing-only format let the first issue raised lead into other issues that members mention. What one person shares will raise certain issues in other group members. As they describe their issues, lead the group to respond. Let the group propel itself in this manner. It is not necessary for you to know exactly where the group will end when the session concludes, since the group process unfolds step-by-step through the session.

3. Discussion-question format. If you are using discussion questions, limit the check-in time to allow discussion of the questions below. These are more

---

Discussion Questions for Week 6

- Can you remember messages from your childhood that pointed you toward perfectionism?
  - ❑ The "almost" message
  - ❑ The zero-defects message
  - ❑ The hard work cover-up message
  - ❑ The idle-hands message
  - ❑ The reach-for-the-stars message
- Have you engaged in perfectionist behavior that has hurt your relationships with other people?
- Do you find yourself caught in the perfectionism/procrastination syndrome?
- Do you let yourself stop and celebrate when something good happens?

---

questions than you will be able to cover in one session. As group members respond to the questions, remember to keep the group operating on a feeling level. Use questions like "How does that make you feel?" Ask group members to respond by choosing one of the emotions from the list on the poster "Feelings."

4. Feeling check. Between 15 and 30 minutes before the session is scheduled to adjourn, conduct a feeling check. Point to the different emotions listed on the poster and ask group members which feelings they are experiencing now.

Encourage members to accept themselves as accepted and greatly loved by God.

Remind the group members to complete the five daily assignments in unit 7 before the next session. Emphasize saying aloud the affirmations each day.

5. Circle of prayer. Encourage group members to ask for God's help in breaking out of the prison of perfectionism.

After the Session

- ❑ Collect the name tags.
- ❑ Mark attendance on the group roster.
- ❑ Record in your journal your thoughts and feelings about the session.
- ❑ Evaluate your skill-building work by answering the following questions. Record appropriate responses in your journal.
  - List occasions in this session when you facilitated one group member's giving feedback to another group member.
  - How much of today's session operated on a feeling level? How much of today's session stayed on a rational level? What part did you play in this balance?
  - What happened in this session that was totally unexpected? How did you respond to it?
  - What did you do in this session to teach group members to help one another?
- ❑ Contact your apprentice or assistant group facilitator to evaluate the session.

Healing Painful Memories

> ➤ **Session Goal**
>
> Group members will be able to discuss painful memories from childhood.

What to Expect

This unit will help group members better understand the need to confront painful childhood memories. During the first session you asked group members to share painful memories from childhood. Perhaps some group members have not yet shared their most painful memories. This unit and the sharing that has taken place in your group in recent weeks may prompt some group members to share at a deeper level during this session.

Group members should be gaining a greater sense of hope that the group process is moving them toward recovery. Look for signs that group members are overcoming the initial grief and pain that confronting the dysfunctional nature of their childhood families caused.

Skill Development

Review the following three skills in preparation for this session.

❏ **1. Communicate acceptance and concern (p. 19).** Accepting a person as she is does not necessarily mean that you agree with the person's values or choices. You can love a person without agreeing with the person. If a person's values need to change, a caring, sympathetic friend is more likely to influence those values than is a judgmental critic.

How do you communicate acceptance and concern? Here are some simple guidelines.

- Listen intently and aggressively.
- When someone shares something emotionally painful, lean toward her. Use facial expressions to show concern. Nod your head. When the person has to stop because the emotion is too strong, say, "I support you."

- When a group member cries and says, "I'm sorry," say: "It's OK to cry in this group. We are here to share your pain."
- After a group member has shared something that makes him feel vulnerable and ashamed, say something like: "I know that sharing what you just shared took a lot of courage. I admire you for being able to share it."
- If a group member condemns the actions or words of another group member who has shared, intervene. Remind members that they are not here to judge one another.

As group members share painful childhood memories, they may feel shame. The shame may not be logical. Listening to a group member's story, you may see the group member as an innocent victim, while the person telling the story feels that the incident somehow was his responsibility. Remember that children in dysfunctional families learn to carry the shame of others. Remember to communicate acceptance even when it seems that the group member's story reveals no obvious need for a special expression of acceptance on your part.

❏ **2. Create a feeling of safety in the group (p. 20).** Adult children need a safe place emotionally. Part of your role as group facilitator is to help create an atmosphere of safety and trust in the group. An important way to create a safe feeling is to enforce boundaries during the group sessions.

As group facilitator, you will enforce boundaries during the sessions. Boundaries are invisible fences that surround an emotionally healthy person. We have physical boundaries. If a casual acquaintance stands three inches from your face while talking with you, you step back because this person has violated your physical space. Sexual boundaries set protective limits on the sexual experiences you choose or reject. Emotional boundaries sound an alarm when someone rages at you or attempts to control your feelings. Spiritual boundaries protect you from unhealthy forms of religion that manipulate you.

Adult children suffer from broken or damaged boundaries. Sexual-abuse victims may have trouble understanding their right to say no. Physical-abuse victims may have an underdeveloped sense of the need and the right to protect themselves from physical harm. An individual who grew up in a dysfunctional family may have trouble shielding himself from unnecessary emotional pain.

Your group needs to be a place where persons can learn to build healthy boundaries. You can assist in this process by enforcing boundaries as group members interact with one another and by respecting group members' boundaries in your interactions with them. Do not permit a group member to act in a verbally abusive way toward another group member. Do not force group members to do or say anything unwillingly. Recognize the difference between gently pushing a group member to a point of discovery and exercising manipulative force, which pushes the individual to behavior that is against his will.

❑ 3. Guide the expression of anger (p. 21).

Before the Session

❑ Review the notes you took on each group member's responses during the first session and pray for each member.
❑ Check the room environment (see p. 35).
❑ Display the poster "Feelings."
❑ If you are using the discussion-question format, you may want to write the discussion questions on a chalkboard or on poster board.
❑ Review the self-evaluation checklist on the inside back cover.

During the Session

1. Arrival. Greet the group members as they arrive; distribute name tags; and start on time.

2. Checking in. Begin by letting the group members check in. (Refer to the inside back cover if needed.)

Start the check-in time by asking, "Does anyone have anything pressing that he or she needs to share today?" or "What happened in your life this past week as a result of our previous session?" Consider using these questions during the check-in period.

Checking In for Week 7

- Is your present behavior being affected by painful memories? If so, how?
  - ❑ Sensing generally that something is wrong
  - ❑ Feeling immobilized by fear
  - ❑ Avoiding certain feelings or situations
  - ❑ Denying reality
- Do you recognize any warning signs of buried traumatic memories?
  - ❑ The feeling of being an adult child but not knowing for sure why
  - ❑ Foggy memories of your whole childhood
  - ❑ Unusual feelings about rooms in houses from childhood
  - ❑ Feedback from other people
  - ❑ Inability to experience certain feelings

In the sharing-only format let the first issue raised lead into issues that other group members mention. What one person shares will raise certain issues in the lives of other group members. As they describe their issues, you can lead the group to respond to them. You can build the whole session around responses to the needs group members identify. Having completed the week's assignments, they will reflect in the issues they raise what they have learned.

3. Discussion-question format. If you are using discussion questions, limit the check-in time to allow discussion of the questions below. These are more questions than you will be able to cover in one session.

As group members respond to the questions, remember to keep the group operating on a feeling level. Use questions like "How does that make you feel?" Ask group members to respond by choosing one of the emotions from the list on the poster "Feelings."

Discussion Questions for Week 7

- What are you afraid of finding in your search for painful memories?
- What is a painful memory that you have not yet shared with the group?

---

4. Feeling check. Between 15 and 30 minutes before the session is scheduled to adjourn, conduct a feeling check. Point to the different emotions listed on the poster and ask group members which feelings they are experiencing now. Remind the group members to complete the five daily assignments in unit 8 before the next session.

5. Circle of prayer. Encourage each group member to thank God for something that happened during today's session. Invite members to pray for the healing of their painful memories.

After the Session

❏ Collect the name tags.
❏ Mark attendance on the group roster.
❏ Record in your journal your thoughts and feelings about the session.
❏ Evaluate your skill-building work by answering the following questions. Record appropriate responses in your journal.
- List one thing you did during the session to communicate acceptance to a group member.
- Do the members of your group feel that the group is a safe place? What have you done to create a feeling of safety?
- Did anyone get in touch with anger during this session? What did you do to facilitate a healthy expression of anger?
❏ Contact your apprentice or assistant group facilitator to evaluate the session.

The Advantages of a Turbulent Past

> ### ➤ Session Goal
>
> Group members will identify and understand positive outcomes that may result from a painful past.

What to Expect

Some members of your group may not be ready to acknowledge that any good has come from their painful childhoods. Be patient with such individuals. Most likely, they are just beginning to get in touch with the pain of the past. Perhaps they have spent their lives telling themselves that their childhoods were not that bad.

Through this study they are now beginning to face the past honestly. Challenging them to see the good in the past may sound like an invitation to revert to denial. Be patient. Let each group member move along on a timetable that is appropriate for him. Push gently while being sensitive to the way each person is responding.

This week's discussion of dysfunctional family roles may lead some group members to a deeper awareness of the dysfunctional nature of their families of origin. Be ready for some group members to take a giant step out of denial about the past as they make new admissions about the true nature of their childhoods.

A challenge for this session is to help group members integrate the spiritual and psychological aspects of their past experiences. As a person begins to confront the emotional pain of her childhood, this new understanding of the past may feel threatening to her faith.

She may perceive that her religious experience has been more the result of control by an authority figure in her life than the result of a free choice she made. Her faith may have involved more compliance than obedience. As she becomes more honest about the pain of her past, she may find that she needs to examine the true nature of her past religious experience.

Help group members understand that a healthy understanding of the past from an emotional/psychological perspective can lead to a deeper faith in Christ, as they learn to make their own free choices for obedience rather than compliant choices based in fear.

Skill Development

Review the following skills in preparation for this session.

❏ **1. Be personally involved without relinquishing leadership (p. 19).** As the facilitator, you need to participate in the group and to share some of your personal struggles. You need to demonstrate vulnerability. At the same time, you are the group facilitator. If you move too deeply into your personal sharing, you may suddenly discover that the group process has stopped because the group no longer has a facilitator.

Another extreme is being detached, assuming the role of a "professional" group facilitator. Your role as group facilitator is not that of a trained expert who has solved all his problems and who shows up each week to help struggling group members with their problems. Your role is that of a fellow struggler, one who also understands emotional pain. Never attempt to create emotions you don't feel or to magnify your emotions to be a good example. The keys are letting yourself get in touch with your feelings and then being honest about them.

❏ **2. Integrate biblical and psychological truth (p. 23).** Sometimes Christians use shallow recitations of biblical truth to hide from the pain of their pasts. The Bible does not call individuals to shallow recitations of its teachings. God calls people to honest self-inventory. As we better understand ourselves, we are better able to obey the deep truths of Scripture.

❏ **3. Read nonverbal communication (p. 25).**

Before the Session

❏ Review the notes you took on each group member's responses during the first session and pray for each member.
❏ Check the room environment (see p. 35).
❏ Display the poster "Feelings."

- ❏ List on posterboard the following dysfunctional family roles or enlarge the illustration on page 63 to poster size: Scapegoat, Lost child, Clown, Placator, Hero, Rebel, Surrogate spouse, Little parent, Little prince/princess.
- ❏ Write on a chalkboard or on poster board the following list of positive results of a difficult childhood: *strong survival instinct, desire for excellence, ability to help others, other.*
- ❏ If you are using the discussion-question format, you may want to write the discussion questions on a chalkboard or on poster board.
- ❏ Review the self-evaluation checklist on the inside back cover.

During the Session

1. Arrival. Greet the group members as they arrive; distribute name tags; and start on time.

2. Checking in. Begin by letting the group members check in.

Start the check-in time by asking, "What happened in your life this past week as a result of our previous session?" Consider using these questions during the check-in period. Refer members to the two posters you prepared.

Checking In for Week 8

- What was your role in your family of origin?
- How did your role in your family of origin affect your childhood? How is it affecting you today?
- Can you name some positive results of your painful childhood?
- Do these positive results have negative side effects? What are they?

In the sharing-only format let the first issue raised lead into issues that other group members mention. What one person shares will raise certain issues in the lives of other group members. As they describe their issues, you can lead the group to respond to them.

You can build the whole session around responses to the needs group members identify. Having completed the week's assignments, group members will reflect what they have learned in the issues they raise.

3. Discussion-question format. If you are using discussion questions, limit the check-in time to allow discussion of the questions below. These are more questions than you will be able to cover in one session.

Discussion Questions for Week 8

- As you think about your childhood, do you have a sense of being wounded? Why?
- As you review the common traits of adult children, do you have a sense of fatalism about your life?
- Do the concepts you are learning in this group seem threatening to your faith? If so, how?
- What have you learned this week to help you move beyond your painful past?

As group members respond to the questions, remember to keep the group operating on a feeling level. Use questions like "How does that make you feel?" Ask group members to respond by choosing one of the emotions from the list on the poster "Feelings."

4. Feeling check. Between 15 and 30 minutes before the session is scheduled to adjourn, conduct a feeling check. Point to the different emotions listed on the poster and ask group members which feelings they are experiencing now. Remind the group members to complete the five daily assignments in unit 9 before the next session.

5. Circle of prayer. Encourage each group member to thank God for something that happened during today's session.

After the Session

- ❏ Collect the name tags.
- ❏ Mark attendance on the group roster.
- ❏ Record in your journal your thoughts and feelings about the session.
- ❏ Evaluate your skill-building work by answering the following questions. Record appropriate responses in your journal.
  - What is one thing you said in today's session that indicated your personal involvement and vulnerability?
  - List three or more strong examples of nonverbal communication that occurred in this session.
- ❏ Contact your apprentice or assistant group facilitator to evaluate the session.

Group Session 9

It's OK to Be Yourself

> ### ➤ Session Goal
>
> Group members will be encouraged to remove emotional masks and to be themselves when they relate to others.

What to Expect

Through this unit group members will learn ways dysfunctional families teach children to wear masks and to assume survival roles that hide the child's true identity. This week group members will receive permission to be themselves.

For some adult children permission to be themselves is not enough. The adult child may say: "I have no idea who I am. My personal self never had a chance to develop. I'm not sure what I like. I don't know what I want." In this unit group members will be challenged to begin deciding who they want to be in areas of confusion about personal identity.

Focus on giving group members permission to be themselves. Each group member should be encouraged to rejoice in his own uniqueness. Look for ways to affirm each group member's individuality.

Help group members to realize how other group members see them. Name specific traits of group members. Act as a mirror for persons who have difficulty seeing their own images.

Help group members get in touch with the grace and love of God. Ultimately, we all need to feel God's permission to be ourselves.

Skill Development

❏ **1. Facilitate feedback (p. 21).** This week's focus is on helping group members know who they are. Encourage group members to help others in the group discover their uniqueness. Adult children often suffer from a clouded self-image.

Help group members help other group members see themselves. Encourage group members to share statements such as "Since we have been meeting as a group, I have come to admire the fact that you …"

❏ **2. Keep the group operating on a feeling level (p. 23).**

Sometimes a certain emotion will hang over the group like a cloud. When you have a sense of such a powerful emotion, it may signal that the whole group is feeling something but is refusing to acknowledge it. Or it may simply be a powerful feeling that most of the members are experiencing at the same time.

In either case it is important for you to call that emotion by name: "I'm feeling a lot of _____ in the room." Ask group members if they sense the same feeling. Ask, "What is this feeling about?" Discuss the origin of the emotion that hangs over the group.

❏ **3. Validate feelings (p. 26).**

Before the Session

❏ Review the notes you took on each group member's responses during the first session and pray for each member.
❏ Check the room environment (see p. 35).
❏ Display the poster "Feelings."
❏ If you are using the discussion-question format, you may want to write the discussion questions on a chalkboard or on poster board.
❏ Review the self-evaluation checklist on the inside back cover.

During the Session

1. Arrival. Greet the group members as they arrive; distribute name tags; and start on time.

2. Checking in. Begin by letting the group members check in.

Start the check-in time by asking, "Does anyone have anything pressing that he or she needs to share today?" or "What happened in your life this past week as a result of our previous session?"

53

In the sharing-only format let the first issue raised lead into issues that other group members mention. What one person shares will raise certain issues in the lives of other group members. As group members describe their issues, you can lead the group to respond to them. You can build the whole session around responses to the needs group members identify. Having completed the week's assignments, they will reflect what they have learned in the issues they raise.

3. Discussion-question format. If you are using discussion questions, limit the check-in time to allow discussion of the questions below. These are more questions than you will be able to cover in one session.

As group members respond to the questions, remember to keep the group operating on a feeling level. Use questions like "How does that make you feel?" and "How did you feel when you heard that?" Ask group members to respond by choosing one of the emotions from the list on the poster "Feelings."

4. Feeling check. Between 15 and 30 minutes before the session is scheduled to adjourn, conduct a feeling check. Point to the different emotions listed on the poster and ask group members which feelings they are experiencing now. Remind the group members to complete the five daily assignments in unit 10 before the next session.

5. Circle of prayer. Encourage each group member to thank God for something that happened during today's session.

After the Session

- ❑ Collect the name tags.
- ❑ Mark attendance on the group roster.
- ❑ Record in your journal your thoughts and feelings about the session.
- ❑ Evaluate your skill-building work by answering the following questions. Record appropriate responses in your journal.
  - What did you do during this session to help group members give feedback to one another?
  - Did this session operate on a feeling level or on an intellectual level? What impact did your leadership have?
  - What makes you feel that the session offered a safe environment in which group members could express their emotions? What impact did your leadership have?
- ❑ Contact your apprentice or assistant group facilitator to evaluate the session.

Group Session 10 | Forgiving the People Who Have Hurt You

> **➤ Session Goal**
>
> Each group member will write a plan for forgiving persons whose actions caused significant childhood pain.

What to Expect

Some group members may have more emotional processing to do before they work on forgiveness. Be careful not to short-circuit the process of forgiveness with a premature push to forgive. A danger at this point would be to push a group member back into shame because he still is struggling with forgiveness. Give group members freedom to process fear, shame, and anger appropriately. Remind those who do not seem ready to forgive that they will need to do so sometime in the future if not now.

Persons who have experienced physical or sexual abuse may have an especially difficult time with forgiveness. Forgiveness may feel like relinquishing power to the perpetrator of the abuse. Help such persons understand that forgiveness does not mean that the perpetrator was justified in his or her behavior. Forgiveness does not mean yielding power to the perpetrator. In fact, forgiveness means removing the perpetrator's power to control through simmering bitterness and fear.

As you approach the final session of your group, some members may express sadness and even fear about the group's end. Group members may make remarks like "I've finally found a safe emotional environment, and it's already ending! We're just getting started." Review "Plan for Follow-up Groups" on page 9 (step 17) for ideas on how to address this issue.

Skill Development

❑ **1. Be willing to confront in love (p. 19).** If a member of your group still is in strong denial about his childhood, such an individual may voice a superficial expression of forgiveness toward his parents while he inwardly harbors deep resentment toward them. Be willing to confront such a person lovingly. Help this person understand the importance of dealing with the bitterness and then moving on to heartfelt forgiveness.

As the group nears the end of the study, you may have only a few more opportunities to help group members who have moved slowly in facing the pain of childhood. Remember that you do not have to "repair" a person who is unwilling to be helped. At the same time, be sensitive to the fact that some of the persons in your group never may be as open as they are now to your constructive confrontation.

❑ **2. Integrate biblical and psychological truth (p. 23).** This unit may offer your best opportunity to integrate biblical and psychological truth in the group process. Forgiveness is at the heart of the good news. Forgiveness is part of the light at the end of the tunnel for adult children.

Use this opportunity to help group members catch a glimpse of God's great love and willingness to forgive. Lift up His example as the one we are to follow.

If group members are not ready to forgive, challenge them to make forgiveness a goal. Help them see that the process of recovery ultimately must lead to forgiving the persons who hurt them as children. Encourage them to look to God for help in forgiving.

Remind group members that an unwillingness to forgive others is like a heavy weight pressing down on the shoulders. An unwillingness to forgive on my part does not make the other person my prisoner as much as it makes me a prisoner of bitterness.

Before the Session

❑ Review the notes you took on each group member's responses during the first session and pray for each member.
❑ Check the room environment (see p. 35).
❑ Display the poster "Feelings."
❑ If you are using the discussion-question format, you may want to write the discussion questions on a chalkboard or on poster board.
❑ Review the self-evaluation checklist on the inside back cover.

During the Session

1. Arrival. Greet the group members as they arrive; distribute name tags; and start on time.

2. Checking in. Begin by letting the group members check in.

Start the check-in time by asking, "Does anyone have anything pressing that he or she needs to share today?" or "What happened in your life this past week as a result of our previous session?" Consider using this question during the check-in period.

Checking In for Week 10

- How has your understanding of forgiveness changed because of this week's study?

In the sharing-only format let the first issue raised lead into issues that other group members mention. What one person shares will raise certain issues in the lives of other group members. As they describe their issues, you can lead the group to respond to them. You can build the whole session around responses to the needs group members identify. Having completed the week's assignments, they will reflect in the issues they raise what they have learned.

3. Discussion-question format. If you are using discussion questions, limit the check-in time to allow discussion of the questions below. These are more questions than you will be able to cover in one session.

Discussion Questions for Week 10

- What roadblocks are keeping you from forgiving the people who have hurt you?
- Describe the kind of forgiveness you need to express toward the people who hurt you as a child.
- Share your plans for forgiving the people who hurt you during childhood.

As group members respond to the questions, remember to keep the group operating on a feeling level. Use questions like "How does that make you feel?" Ask group members to respond by choosing one of the emotions from the list on the poster "Feelings."

4. Feeling check and follow-up. Ask group members how they feel about the fact that the group soon will be coming to an end. You may find that the members of your group feel sad and concerned about the group's disbanding.

Help group members process the grief they feel about the group's end. Encourage them to talk about their feelings.

Here are some suggestions that can help.

Follow-up Options

- Review group–Your existing Face-to-Face group could agree to meet together for 12 more weeks. Members could review content in *Making Peace with Your Past* and use the sharing-only format for the group sessions. This would be a good time to share leadership and provide on-the-job training for potential leaders.
- *Moving Beyond Your Past* group–Your group could agree to stay together for another 12 weeks and complete the follow-up to *Making Peace with Your Past—Moving Beyond Your Past*.
- New content/same group–Your existing group could agree to stay together for another 12 weeks and use *Search for Significance* LIFE® Support Group Series Edition or *Untangling Relationships: A Christian Perspective on Codependency*, or *Breaking the Cycle of Hurtful Family Experiences* as additional input for group members.
- New Face-to-Face groups–Members can go through the Face-to-Face process in new groups. These groups could include both experienced and first-time participants.
- Specialized support groups–You could provide specialized support groups for personal issues such as divorce recovery, grief, abuse recovery; or you could provide 12-Step support groups for additions such as chemical dependency, codependency, or eating disorders.
- Discipleship group–Members could move to a discipleship course such as *Experiencing God*, *Disciple's Prayer Life*, or *MasterLife*.
- Leader training group–Some selected members could move into a leader training track beginning with a course like *WiseCounsel: Skills for Lay Counseling*.

Whatever decision the group makes about an ongoing focus, make sure the group clearly has a stated purpose, a set of agreements, and a defined life span. It's good for a group to reevaluate its purpose and direction about once a quarter.

If the group is interested in continuing, gather preliminary input from the group and plan to discuss the group's future more fully during the last session.

5. Circle of prayer. Encourage each group member to thank God for something that happened during today's session.

After the Session

❏ Collect the name tags.
❏ Mark attendance on the group roster.
❏ Record in your journal your thoughts and feelings about the session.
❏ Evaluate your skill-building work by answering the following questions. Record appropriate responses in your journal.
  • Describe an incident in today's session or in a recent session when you lovingly confronted a group member. What was the group member's response? What did you learn from this experience?
  • What did you do during this session to integrate biblical and psychological truth?
❏ Contact your apprentice or assistant group facilitator to evaluate the session.

Coming to Terms with the Blessing

> ### ➤ Session Goal
>
> Group members will receive the blessings of others.

What to Expect

Some group members may feel a sense of panic as they realize that the study is almost over. This panic will be especially acute for persons who have wanted to bring a particular issue before the group but have been afraid to do so. Their ambivalent feelings will intensify when they realize that the study is ending. Encourage them to share during this session.

Other group members will feel grief over the fact that the group is about to disband. Help these individuals identify their feelings. Give them an opportunity to work through their feelings as part of the group process.

Offer ideas for continuing the recovery process after the study is over. Options include reading some of the books on recovery listed on page 18 of this guide, joining another support group, or finding another person interested in recovery with whom to meet on a regular basis.

Skill Development

Review the following two skills in preparation for this session.

❏ **1. Communicate acceptance and concern (p. 19).** This session offers a powerful opportunity to communicate unconditional acceptance in the group. In the section "Sharing the Blessing" you will find guidelines for an exercise that gives group members a specific way to bless (or affirm) one another.

Even before this session ends, give special attention to communicating acceptance to group members. Remember that accepting a person as he is does not necessarily mean that you agree with the person's values or choices. It does mean that you are willing to love this person now without waiting for certain conditions to be met.

Recognize the destructive power of shame in the lives of group members. It is hoped that members have won major victories over shame during the study. However, shame-based identities do not vanish overnight. Be alert to opportunities to cut through shame and to affirm persons in the group.

❏ **2. Teach group members to help one another (p. 25).** As mentioned, the exercise described in the section "Sharing the Blessing" will allow members to bless one another.

Use this exercise to encourage group members to help one another. At the beginning of the session tell group members that they will share blessings with one another at the close of the session.

Throughout the session work on letting go of the group. Give members extra time to say what you would have said. As much as possible, let the group members help one another without your intervention.

Before the Session

❏ Review the notes you took on each group member's responses during the first session and pray for each member.
❏ Check the room environment (see p. 35).
❏ Display the poster "Feelings."
❏ If you are using the discussion-question format, you may want to write the discussion questions on a chalkboard or on poster board.
❏ Review the self-evaluation checklist on the inside back cover.

During the Session

1. Arrival. Greet the group members as they arrive; distribute name tags; and start on time.

2. Checking in. Begin by letting the group members check in. Start the check-in time by asking, "Does anyone have anything pressing that he or she needs to share today?" or "What happened in your life this past week as a result of our previous session?" Consider using these questions during the check-in period.

In the sharing-only format let the first issue raised lead into issues that other group members mention. What one person shares will raise certain issues in the lives of other group members. As they describe their issues, you can lead the group to respond to them. You can build the whole session around responses to the needs group members identify. Having completed the week's assignments, they will reflect what they have learned in the issues they raise.

3. Discussion-question format. If you are using discussion questions, limit the check-in time to allow discussion of the questions below. These are more questions than you will be able to cover in one session.

Discussion Questions for Week 11

- What persons in your life caused you to feel that you were not blessed?
- How did these persons communicate a withheld blessing to you?
- Did you receive a limited blessing? What were the limits or conditions?
- Was a brother or a sister in your family blessed in a way that you were not blessed? Describe the situation.
- Are you still seeking the blessing from your family of origin? How?
- What are you going to do about the blessing in your life?
- Have you allowed yourself to grieve for the missing blessing?

As group members respond to the questions, remember to keep the group operating on a feeling level. Use questions like "How does that make you feel?" Ask group members to respond by choosing one of the emotions from the list on the poster "Feelings."

4. Sharing the blessing. About 30 minutes before the session is scheduled to adjourn, lead the group in a blessing exercise.

- Ask half of the group members to sit in a circle.
- Instruct the other members to stand behind the seated members.
- Ask each person standing to lean toward the seated group member and to whisper a blessing. The blessing could be an affirmation, like "In Christ it is OK for you to be yourself." Or it might be a personal expression, like "During the study I have grown to appreciate your honesty."
- After each seated person has received a blessing, the persons who are standing should rotate so that each one is standing behind a new person.
- Each standing person again will share a blessing with the seated person.
- Repeat this process until everyone sitting has received a blessing from everyone standing.
- Then, to repeat the cycle, the persons who are seated should trade places with the persons standing.

Remind members to complete the five review assignments in unit 12 before the next session.

5. Circle of prayer. Encourage each group member to thank God for something that happened during today's session.

After the Session

- ❏ Collect the name tags.
- ❏ Mark attendance on the group roster.
- ❏ Record in your journal your thoughts and feelings about the session.
- ❏ Evaluate your skill-building work by answering the following questions. Record appropriate responses in your journal.
    - What did you do during this session to communicate acceptance and concern?
    - What did you do to teach group members to help one another?
- ❏ Contact your apprentice or assistant group facilitator to evaluate the session.

Reflection and Direction

> ## ➤ Session Goal

Group members will express gratitude for the group process and will demonstrate a commitment to continue their recovery.

Discussion Questions for Week 12

- What goals have you accomplished during the past 11 weeks?
- Which of your goals for the group were not accomplished?
- In what ways has your thinking changed during the study?

What to Expect

Expect joy, a sense of "I have found help; I am getting better," as group members reflect on the progress they have made in the study. Also expect some sadness, even fear, as group members think about the group's disbanding. The sadness comes from ending a positive experience of emotional intimacy. Members also may fear regressing to earlier patterns of emotional dysfunction once they lose the support of the group.

Expect to receive affirmation as group members talk about the progress they have made. Be prepared to credit God with the healing that has taken place.

Before the Session

❑ Review the notes you took on each group member's responses during the first session and pray for each member.
❑ Check the room environment (see p. 35).
❑ Display the poster "Feelings."
❑ If you are using the discussion-question format, you may want to write the discussion questions on a chalkboard or on poster board.
❑ Review the self-evaluation checklist on the inside back cover.

During the Session

1. Arrival. Greet the group members as they arrive; distribute name tags; and start on time.

2. Review. Build this session on a discussion of each group member's responses to the questions in day 5 of unit 12 in the member's book. Ask each group member to respond to the following questions.

Allow each group member to share responses to all three questions before proceeding to the next group member. As each person shares, glance at the notes you made during the first session. Help individuals remember goals they shared during the first session but have forgotten. Be ready to affirm each group member by making personal comments about positive changes you have seen. Some group members may not realize that they have accomplished the goals they set. Help them recognize and acknowledge their progress.

3. Plans for recovery. Ask each group member to summarize a plan for recovery. The questions that outline a recovery plan are found in day 5 of unit 12 in the member's book (p. 217). As each member shares, encourage and commend each person and make helpful suggestions.

4. What next? If you plan to offer the group the option of continuing for another 12-week period, allow time to discuss the next phase. Reserve this discussion for the end of the session. The group's future plans should not be the session's main topic. Build the session around the discussion suggested in steps 2 and 3 above.

Discuss the following details when planning the group's next step.

- Who will lead the group?
  ❑ A selected facilitator
  ❑ Rotating leadership among group members
- When and where will the group meet? When will the next session be?
- How often will the group meet?
- What will be the purpose of the group?
- Will you use the same covenant you used for this group? If not, what agreements will you make?

- Will the group use study material?
- When will the new group evaluate its plans beyond the next 12 weeks?

If time for this discussion runs out, the new group can use the first session of the next 12 to complete plans.

5. Circle of prayer. Encourage each group member to thank God for the group experience and for the work He has done in each life.

After the Session

❏ Collect the name tags.
❏ Mark attendance on the group roster.
❏ Record in your journal your thoughts and feelings about the session.
❏ Contact your apprentice or assistant group facilitator to evaluate the session.

FEELINGS

ANGER! FEAR

joy

GUILT LONELINESS

Other?

SADNESS

Dysfunctional Family Roles

Face-to-Face Support Group Affirmations

- I accept God's love for me.
- God is in control.
- Through Jesus Christ I am clean in God's sight.
- I release my fears to Jesus.
- I claim the joy of being God's child.
- Because God loves me, it is OK to be incomplete.

- I accept God's healing of the painful memories of my past.
- No matter what happens, I trust that God is working for my good.
- In Christ it is OK for me to be myself.
- Because God has forgiven me, I can forgive others.
- I am blessed.

Face-to-Face Support Group Affirmations

- I accept God's love for me.
- God is in control.
- Through Jesus Christ I am clean in God's sight.
- I release my fears to Jesus.
- I claim the joy of being God's child.
- Because God loves me, it is OK to be incomplete.

- I accept God's healing of the painful memories of my past.
- No matter what happens, I trust that God is working for my good.
- In Christ it is OK for me to be myself.
- Because God has forgiven me, I can forgive others.
- I am blessed.

Face-to-Face Support Group Affirmations

- I accept God's love for me.
- God is in control.
- Through Jesus Christ I am clean in God's sight.
- I release my fears to Jesus.
- I claim the joy of being God's child.
- Because God loves me, it is OK to be incomplete.

- I accept God's healing of the painful memories of my past.
- No matter what happens, I trust that God is working for my good.
- In Christ it is OK for me to be myself.
- Because God has forgiven me, I can forgive others.
- I am blessed.

Face-to-Face Support Group Affirmations

- I accept God's love for me.
- God is in control.
- Through Jesus Christ I am clean in God's sight.
- I release my fears to Jesus.
- I claim the joy of being God's child.
- Because God loves me, it is OK to be incomplete.

- I accept God's healing of the painful memories of my past.
- No matter what happens, I trust that God is working for my good.
- In Christ it is OK for me to be myself.
- Because God has forgiven me, I can forgive others.
- I am blessed.

You have permission to copy this page for use in Face-to-Face Support Groups.